The Buddha's Wish for the World

On the Occasion of the 750th Memorial

for Shinran Shonin (1173-1263)

MONSHU KOSHIN OHTANI

American Buddhist Study Center Press
New York

Edited and Published by
American Buddhist Study Center Press, New York, NY

In Collaboration with
Buddhist Study Center, Honolulu, HI and
Buddhist Education Center (BEC), Anaheim, CA

First Edition 2009

The Buddha's Wish for the World

Based on the Japanese Title
Ashita ni wa kogan arite,
Tokyo: Kadokawa shoten, 2003

Translated by Wayne S. Yokoyama

Library of Congress Cataloging in Publication Data
Ohtani, Monshu Koshin
The Buddha's Wish for the World / Monshu Koshin Ohtani
ISBN 978-0-9764594-2-2

This Book is Printed with Soy Inks on 10% Recycled Paper

Printed in the United States of America
Designed by Arlene Kato

"Monshu" is the title of the head of the Nishi Hongwanji. Literally it means
"Master of the Gate." The present Monshu is a direct descendent of Shinran Shonin,
the founder of Shin Buddhism. In Japanese, an honorific prefix "Go" is added to the word
"Monshu" which shows respect. Therefore, you will sometimes see the Monshu referred
to as "Gomonshu," but the actual word and title is simply "Monshu."

The Buddha's Wish for the World

On the Occasion of the 750th Memorial

for Shinran Shonin (1173-1263)

MONSHU KOSHIN OHTANI

Contents

MONSHU KOSHIN OHTANI

Greetings

Nearly 800 years have elapsed since Shinran Shonin revealed to us the Jodo Shinshu teaching. I believe that now it is time for us to discover how we can accept and appreciate it amidst the great changes going on in society. In the contemporary world, we are confronted with a constant stream of distressing problems. Buddhism teaches us to critically examine the overall direction of modern civilization. It reveals to us that these problems arise from human greed and desires that have only increased in proportion to every advance in science and technology. To my mind, this is one of the many things that we ought to learn from the Buddha Dharma.

As one studies the Buddha Dharma, these things become clearer in time, though at first it may not always be easy to see how it applies to one's way of life. Since this book was originally intended for the Japanese reader, I am afraid that for those persons who are more comfortable with English than Japanese, there may also be portions that will seem perplexing at first. I hope that you will take this as an opportunity to learn and gain insight into the Japanese way of thinking and customs.

On this occasion, I wish to gratefully acknowledge the many people, both named and anonymous, who assisted with the preparation of this work. This book, *The Buddha's*

Wish for the World, would not have come into existence if it were not for the dedicated efforts of Mr. Hoshin Seki of New York, Reverend Michio Tokunaga of Kyoto, and translator Wayne S. Yokoyama, who took it upon themselves to see to its publication.

Koshin Ohtani
Monshu of the Nishi Hongwanji
Kyoto
Spring 2009

Foreword

To read *The Buddha's Wish for the World* is to feel enfolded within that wish, which the author so deeply feels to be expressed in the vision of the original compassionate vow of the Bodhisattva Dharmakara, who eventually became the Infinite Light Amitabha Buddha. *The Land of Bliss Sutra* describes the Buddha-world he created as an ideal environment in which to free all beings from suffering. That bliss-world is far away from us, from our perspective, as misknowing beings trapped in a highly imperfect material world where we struggle to subsist. But from the perspective of the enlightened beings in that world, our world is right there, our whole universe; as if a grain of sand or a subatomic energy. Hence, their compassion can enfold us all and all our doings and seek to turn us from our self-defeating egocentric ways toward the self-fulfilling way of wisdom and altruism.

If the foundation of Monshu Ohtani's vision is this cosmic sense of the omnicompetent presence of the infinite light and life Buddha, his wisdom reaches out to us by sharing with us his clear perception of freedom and goodness in the most ordinary places of thought and life. He affirms the central insight of all forms of Buddhism with his statement, "'I am right!' is always the problem, the root of all problems."

He has a sensitive alertness of how to perform the virtues in daily life by being self-aware of the pitfalls of egotism and self-involvement. He gives the wise precept; "Keep that mirror reflecting our frailty handy!" And he reminds us about the seven gifts that require no possessions: 1. The gift of gentle eyes, looking at others kindly. 2. The gift of a smile and kind expressions. 3. The gift of words, speaking kindly to others. 4. The gift of the physical body. Acting properly yourself, and treating others with respect. 5. The gift of heart, touching others with a heart full of love. 6. The gift of a resting place, offering others a place to sit and rest. 7. The gift of shelter and lodging, providing others with a room or warm place to stay.

And he tells us about ways of speech that express the world of bliss in this world of dew; "a simple greeting acknowledging our common humanity, a more elaborate utterance such as those of aesthetic appreciation or voicing a shared situation of concern." He shows us how you can reach out to another human being by "gently pushing open the gate surrounding your heart."

Monshu Ohtani reports how, in Japan, under the benevolent influence of Buddhism, a sign on a temple wall lists a set of rules for hearing (which applies as well to reading, especially this wise book). "1. You should listen as if you are listening for the very first time. 2. You should listen as if the message is for you alone. 3. You should listen as if this is the last time you will ever do so in your life." And he promises us that, "when we let these words enter and soften our hearts, we will one day find ourselves not sighing over the tediousness of our lives. We will find ourselves seeing each moment of this life as precious, and to be cherished."

In the climactic moment of the book, the Monshu Ohtani refers to his illustrious ancestor, reporting how, for Shinran Shonin (1173-1263), the "entrusting heart was the sole cause of attaining Birth in the Pure Land and achieving awakening, satori there." He then describes this entrusting heart so beautifully; "when we put ourselves in the situation where we leave everything to the compassion of Amida Buddha, it is then that a human being is liberated by the entrusting heart as the prime cause. It is through receiving Amida Buddha's heart of true wisdom and compassion that we feel our imperfect selves being supported and held. An indescribable feeling of relief and joy thus arises. When we let this entrusting heart take wing, it expresses itself as the Nembutsu of Namo-Amida-Butsu that we receive from Amida Buddha, the Buddha of Infinite Light and Life."

And I cannot help but quote as well one of his most beautiful passages; "All things, the water and the air included, are linked together, one thing encircling and being encircled by the other. The mountain and the river bestow us with so many blessings. When the light of Amida Buddha shines on us, we are linked together as lives worthy of compassion, worthy of being liberated from ourselves. All things on earth, all things in the universe, are in the fold of this greater life force linking us all."

I am honored to have the opportunity to welcome this

wonderful book of my old friend, the Monshu Koshin Ohtani, with its range of observations of life and liberation, from the tiny but utterly significant moments in ordinary life, of the turning of the mind from egotism to altruistic heart's entrustment to the vast and beautiful vision of the immanence of the all-enfolding universal compassion of Amida Buddha.

Robert "Tenzin" Thurman
President, Tibet House, US
Jey Tsong Khapa Professor of Buddhism,
    Columbia University

Tell me friend,
why do you suppose
we are alive?

1

Why do you suppose we are alive?

Once you start thinking about it, there is no end. The more we want our life to continue on, the more that desire itself becomes the seed of despair. In this sense, human beings are caught in a difficult situation. It would not be overstating the case to say that the whole of human suffering starts from this one question of why we are alive.

Is there, then, an answer to this question?

The short answer would be no, there is no easy answer we can find. It would seem that man was born into life to seek an answer to this question.

Although an answer may not appear during the course of a single day, as long as the strength to contemplate the matter remains within you, the beauty of the human experience lies in the very fact that we struggle with the question of how to live a meaningful life.

Those who are in the midst of a difficult period in their lives may protest, asking, "Of what good is such advice?" I would suggest that we not rush our answer, and instead, take the time to consider what *living* means.

Your life is a gift
wished into existence

2

What is the meaning invested in your name?

When I was born, my parents gave me a name. My first name is Koshin. The first part, Ko, was added to my name when I was ordained as a priest at age 15. My name from childhood is Makoto, which is also pronounced Shin. My father chose the name Makoto, meaning "true," because he wanted me to be a person who would lead a life free of pretence and dishonesty; one who aspires for the truth. I came to be called Makoto because from the very first moment of my life my parents had this wish for me.

And so I grew up with everyone around me calling me Makoto. It is the same for everyone. We grow up being called by a name that is invested with some kind of wish for our lives.

In our temple, when a child is born, we have a ceremony for the baby's first visit to the temple, called *hatsumairi*. The first visit to the temple symbolizes the recognition on the part of the family that this new life has been born into the folds of the Buddha's wishes for the child, and also reaffirms the intent of those surrounding the newborn to raise the child as the child of the Buddha. The child who is brought to the temple on this first occasion is cradled in the arms of the parents and surrounded by the smiling faces of the family. The family members, talking to the baby (who does not understand what the words mean), put their hands together. Seated before the Buddha, they make a wish that the baby will grow up to be a good child and go through life full of happiness.

Another purpose of the baby's first visit is to remind us that throughout our lives we too have been the recipients of the many wishes of others. No one has lived up to this point in life by his or her efforts alone. All of us embrace in our hearts the many wishes that people have made for us. In this way, we have received the wishes of our parents, our grandparents, those all around us, and our society.

3

Like all of us, you have been granted the chance to live

In front of my house, there is a sequoia tree that has grown so large it seems to pierce the sky. In 1951, a University of California professor named Dr. Ralph W. Chaney came to Japan to promote the *metasequoia* and planted one at our temple, the Nishi Hongwanji. I was 6 years old at the time. Ever since then, it has grown tall, dropping its leaves every autumn and sprouting buds come spring. Despite Kyoto's cold winter and hot, humid summer, it has somehow managed to thrive. Sometimes, when I see this tree, I find myself lost in thought. Seeing it sporting fresh green leaves or its form flecked with snow, it would sometimes give me courage. I would find myself thinking, "I guess

Metasequoia photo by Monshu Koshin Ohtani

me and you are growing up together." On this great earth, we live surrounded by friends. This is what I thought as I looked at this tree that said not a word. It is at such times that I sense this tree has a wish for me.

During the Edo period, a poet named Issa (1763-1828) composed the following poem.

takenoko mo	Even the lowly bamboo shoot
nanoru ka	Proclaims to all the world:
yui ga dokuson to	"Truly, I alone am the Honored One!"

When the bamboo shoot first pokes out its head, it is not so much its cuteness as the bearing with which it carries itself that wins us over. Issa must have noticed its commanding presence and related it to the event of Shakyamuni Buddha's birth. He didn't just plop it down at the market for so many pennies a pound. Issa saw in the bamboo shoot another existence living the same life that we all live. He sensed that the same life force that resided in Shakyamuni Buddha was at work in the bamboo shoot and expressed this significance with the words, "Truly, I alone am the Honored One!"

❧

Issa also has another poem that reads,

Namo Amida	Namo Amida:
Butsu no katayori	Message from the Buddha
naku ka kana	Buzzed me via mosquito

"Message from the Buddha" means the mosquito was the agent of the Buddha. The Buddha has the mosquito convey the message of the Nembutsu, the saying of the name of Amida Buddha, to Issa. "Hey Issa, yo!" says the mosquito, "Say that Nembutsu of yours for me!" What might have actually happened was the mosquito bit Issa, who then swatted him with his hand. But that tiny life form connected Issa to the Buddha from whom Issa received the wish that the Buddha hoped to convey. And so, this verse came into existence.

Whether fauna, flora, mountain, river, or work of art flowing up from out of the well of human emotions; what we can sense in all of these is the Buddha's wish for us.

The heart of the matter is we humans turn our backs whenever duty calls and protest that it is not our responsibility. "How come I am the only one who has to do this?" "It is not like I chose to be born in this place." "I didn't do anything wrong." As long as we respond to a situation in this way, we can never get rid of the nagging feeling that the world is unfair or that we are dissatisfied with our lives. We lose sight of the wish the Buddha places on us; we get frustrated with things that do not go the way we expect, and with people who do not do as we say. When we get swept away by our own desires—putting ourselves at the center of everything—we delude ourselves into believing that all of life should serve us.

All of us live life in this problematic way, with our hearts easily upset. When we are swept along in this way, we lose perspective on our lives and become filled with regret as life passes us by.

If we honestly see that this is the way we have been living, we should stop and recall the wishes that the Buddha places on us. In those wishes, we will be sure to discover the meaning of life as a whole.

We all like to put ourselves first

4

So, where are all the good guys?

There is a Japanese saying, "It takes a house full of good people to get all riled up like this." At first, it might seem to go against our common sense, so what does it mean?

Here is a story of what happened to one family.

One day, a mother was just about to start her housework. She moved the precious vase that the father loved so much from the alcove to the corridor facing the garden, and began to clean the room. When her son came home early from school, he knocked the vase over and broke it.

"Oh, I was just trying to get things tidied up before everyone came home and now look what you did," the mother cried. Then she scolded her son, asking, "Why didn't you notice it was there?"

"What do you mean?" the boy asked, talking back to his mother. "You shouldn't have put it there in the first place." He felt he was not to blame, since it was she who had put it there.

"You better apologize to your father when he comes home," the mother continued.

To which the boy shot back, "Me, apologize? Mom, you're the one who should be apologizing!"

In the meantime, it grew late in the day and the father came home. What do you suppose the father said when he heard what had happened? Did he get angry and say, "What a stupid thing to do with something so valuable!" Did he blame the mother and say, "That's what happens when you move things around like that." Or did he scold his son and say, "You're doing dumb things like this all the time. It's because you're so careless that things like this happen."

In fact, the father simply said, "Oh well, things break, not much you can do about it."

When the mother and the son heard these words, they suddenly realized how busy each of them had been loudly proclaiming, "I am right," and were taken aback. If the father had brandished his authority and gotten angry, as we might well have expected him to do, no doubt the mother and the son would each have continued to press their cases. The father might have had every reason to be upset over the loss of his precious vase, but when he said this, both mother and son were able to reflect upon themselves.

Both of them apologized to the father saying, "I should really have been more careful where I put it," and "No, I'm the one to blame. I was careless. I'm sorry."

CR

Shinran Shonin admonishes us not to be slaves to such thinking as, "Oh, how good and clever I am." When we are possessed by the idea that "I am right," we become arrogant and do not turn an ear to what others have to say. Shinran Shonin warns us against this kind of mentality.

The opening statement to this essay, "It takes a house full of good people to get all riled up like this," points to the person who thinks that "I'm the good guy." When we have that kind of attitude, "I'm the good guy," then the idea that "I'm right and not mistaken" asserts itself, and we become inflexible in our views. This sets the stage for a conflict of opinions.

Thinking that "I am right" works out perfectly well for each of us, to the degree that we remain firmly rooted in the position that "I was right in what I did," or "After all I did for you." We do not recognize how to turn off that "I am right" attitude. Our way of thinking might work out well for us, to protect ourselves with it, but it does not take into consideration the position of the person with whom we are dealing.

When two people insist on what is best "for me," it will only end in struggle. This is true, whether we are talking about a family quarrel or a war between two countries. The whole world is made up of a network of people who are intricately intertwined. When we insist on having our own way, someone else will be put out.

Whenever we think of ourselves as "the good," no matter how much we may think this to be true, this is always a case of exaggerated self-importance. Whenever we think of ourselves as being the good guy, we will always run the risk of falling into that kind of trap.

In reality, it is virtually impossible for us to admit our shortcomings to others. We instinctively want to protect ourselves and we are inclined to do only what is best for ourselves. Human beings, it would seem, are just like that.

Rather than insisting, "I am the good guy" and brandishing

the sword of authority in order to turn things in our favor, if we are open to our shortcomings and open our hearts to those around us, saying, "I am sorry, I was wrong," then there would be far less conflict taking place in our relations with others. Whichever society it may be, this point would seem to be universally true.

5

When we delve into our own past, we know there is no one who is totally pure

We have been talking about the good guys, so now let us think about the bad.

In my school of Buddhism, there is a point we like to make about "an evil one as the true object of compassion." Some of the things Shinran Shonin was fond of saying were compiled by a disciple in a book called the *Tannisho*. In that work, there is a section in which Shinran Shonin explains that it is the evil person who is saved through the compassion of Amida Buddha. This is generally referred to as "the evil person is the true object of the compassion of the Buddha" teaching in Jodo Shinshu.

In this case, the expression, "the evil person," is very different from what is usually meant by an evil person. The evil person is not merely a person who has sinned or broken the law or done something immoral.

Before explaining what this means, let us touch briefly on Buddhist history.

Shakyamuni Buddha perceived that the worries and suffering that tormented people had their source in *klesa*, or blind passions. These klesa interfere with our sense of peace and quiet by sending up disturbing thoughts of desire and attachment. He concluded that if such unwholesome feelings as anger and jealousy were removed, the worries and suffering they generated would also be banished from our lives.

That is why the disciples of Shakyamuni selected as their path of choice the way of the ascetic monk. The tradition of asceticism is one that has a long history in India, going back to ancient times. Leaving the home life and bidding farewell to family, the monk sets out to live his life alone. By these means, the heart finds peace, as the monk polishes the mirror of wisdom and leads a life severed from the desires and attachments of worldly life. In order to live, he makes rounds of the villages with begging bowl in hand to obtain the food he needs. Roaming from village to village, the monk takes no place as his permanent abode. At times, the monk will join with other monks and gather in a communal setting, called the *sangha*, where no personal possessions are allowed.

However, the number of people who can pursue such a way of life are few and far between. The reality is that the vast majority of us are unable to pursue the ascetic life. If this means all of us will not be saved from our blind passions, then that would be most troublesome indeed. The Pure Land Buddhist teachings arose from such questions.

The Pure Land teaching declares that it is not in this present world but in the next one, that is, in the life hereafter, that we pursue the religious path leading to *satori*, or enlightenment.

While Shinran Shonin was thoroughly grounded in this tenet of the Pure Land teaching, his experiences brought him to further develop the idea. In his view, it is not only in the next life that dramatic developments occur; he contends that there is a path whereby people come to be liberated in this world as well.

All of us have some form of klesa. Most of us lead ordinary lives, with families and jobs. This makes us less amenable to the life of ascetic practice. What then are we to do to be liberated in this world? This question is the starting point of the Pure Land teaching of Jodo Shinshu, which contends that it is through the compassion of Amida Buddha that we realize liberation.

Shinran Shonin practiced a life of ascetic existence for 20 years on Mount Hiei. Even though he immersed himself in practice day and night, those blind passions remained; he could feel them in his bones.

In Buddhism, there are precepts that a person must follow and never break. There is the view that a person who breaks any of the precepts is regarded as an evil one, a person held in the grips of klesa.

For instance, one precept states that one must not kill any living thing. However, in order for us to live as human beings, we must take the lives of the various plants and animals that we eat. Even those of us who are vegetarians have to take the lives of plants. When we think of it in this way, there is no way that we can live without taking life. In short, all of us are "evil" for breaking this precept.

Shinran Shonin was a person who could neither rid himself of his blind passions nor stop breaking precepts, and yet he came to realize that there was a path of liberation open to him. He thus extolled the view that it is the ordinary people afflicted with klesa—that is, those of us who live out our lives drifting on the sea of blind desires, unable to stem the tide of our blind passions—who, through an epic encounter with the compassion of Amida Buddha, are truly brought to our senses and made to realize the negative tendencies of our ways. Such a person is the one who at last comes to be liberated. This is the teaching that the evil ones are the true objects of the compassion of the Buddha.

According to the words of Shinran Shonin,

> Even a good person attains birth in the Pure Land,
> so it goes without saying that an evil person will.

— *Collected Works of Shinran (CWS), Vol. 1*, P. 663

When we come to our senses and take a good hard look at ourselves, we find that there is no one who is not afflicted with blind passions. When we delve into our own past, we know there is no one who is truly a good person, no one who is innocent and totally pure.

6

It's only natural to have desires, there's no need to suppress them

I want this. I want that.

Desires—everyone has them. When we think that our will to live is essentially rooted in our desires, it is no easy matter to simply do away with them.

From day one, we would be unable to live if we denied ourselves the search for the basic necessities of food, clothing, and shelter.

In India, 2,500 years ago, under the motto of "three robes, one bowl," the homeless ascetic would make do with three kinds of robes and a begging bowl. That was possible because of the warm climatic conditions of the region, as well as the supportive social conditions of that time.

This becomes impossible in regions where there are wide fluctuations in heat and cold. Moreover, in the present world, where people obtain goods by monetary exchange, one cannot possibly manage without money.

In short, what we mean by the basic necessities depends largely on which region we are talking about. It is difficult to draw a line between what is within the realm of necessity and what goes beyond it.

In Buddhism, since ancient times, human desires have been the subject of strict scrutiny. Our desires, at times, bind and fetter us. At other times, our desires make us view other life forms as nothing more than prey, causing us to inflict suffering upon them.

But Shakyamuni did not think simply to suppress his desires. He recommended that we neither subject ourselves to extreme asceticism nor indulge in rank hedonism, but instead aspire to tread the Middle Way in the spirit of moderation.

There is a saying, "He whose desires are few, knows satisfaction." This is not an admonition to stoically deny one's desires. Nor is it a sign to indulge ourselves. The point is knowing what it means to be satisfied by moderating our desires and wanting less.

As human beings, we always think of ourselves first and tend to be swept along by the stream of thinking what is best for us. Without a sense of satisfaction, though, no matter how much money we make or how nice a place we live in, we will always want more; there seems to be no stopping this greed.

In this regard, the sutras speak of the moderation of desires by an analogy to a stringed instrument. When the strings are strung too loose, it is slack and produces no sound; when strung too tight, it is creaky and the strings will break. When the strings are strung just right, it will produce a good sound.

So too, it is impossible for people to live by repressing their desires. At the same time, if we let down our guard, our lives will sound rather slack. When our desires are moderately strung, then our lives, like the stringed instrument, will start to produce beautiful notes.

In Buddhism, there is a set of five basic precepts, or admonitions, that the lay practitioners are expected to live by. They include: no taking of life; no stealing; no illicit relations; no telling of lies; and no consuming of alcohol.

Such precepts or admonitions are not held in the teaching of Jodo Shinshu. This is because we are unable to live without breaking these precepts. This of course does not mean we are free to do whatever we want.

Shinran Shonin tells us that all of us, whoever we might be, will be saved. This is because Amida Buddha does not set any conditions for our liberation. With this tenet as the bottom line, there is no need to bind us with words of admonition by saying there is something that we are forbidden to do.

Originally, the precepts were what the seekers intuited and freely placed upon themselves; it was not something they were forced to do. It was out of their own free will that they decided to refrain from certain actions and things. Here, the thoughts of Shinran Shonin are similar.

There is no reason to suppress desires. The problem is whether you, yourself, can tell if those desires are satisfied or not.

Besides the desire for money and possessions, there is the desire for fame, the desire to cling to status, or the desire to wrest political power. There is no end to the list of things human beings desire to have.

We might say that these desires are, to express it differently, a form of ambition, to improve ourselves. Just by changing the words, it sounds much better. If this invests us with the power to live, there is no denying it. But one false step and it all re-verts back to what they truly are: the things we want, so as to put ourselves first.

What is our final assessment on these desires that come welling up in us?

Think of times when such desires were fulfilled. Were there not times when others, following in the wake of our success, were made to suffer, while seeing their own dreams fall short? Whenever our self-centered desires well up, it creates condi-tions of friction somewhere else. Stop there and ask yourself: Am I or am I not a musical instrument producing a beautiful sound?

7

Trace your anger and hatred back to their source in your desires

Our feelings of anger and hatred are also among our wicked tendencies.

If we consider why we harbor feelings of hatred toward others, it is because they do not do what we want.

Thoughts well up within our hearts such as, "Oh, what a terrible person he is! Why do you suppose he is doing that?" or "Why is he saying that?" That is what happens when some-one says or does something that is contrary to what *you* expect.

It makes you feel frustrated and unhappy. When you are un-happy and fed up because things did not turn out as planned, its source is in your desires.

The more you start thinking, "My way of thinking is right" or "Of course I am right in what I want to do," the more you feel you have to reject your tormentor, and your dislike for that person soon comes to dominate your relationship.

If those feelings of your being good and right were not there, those flames of hatred would not have flared up in the first place.

The same is true of anger. "She did not do what she was supposed to. Oh, I am so angry with her!" If we think we are in the right and what the other person did was wrong, then we feel angry.

Another example is the person who says, "Oh, I am so an-gry at the world." In this case, one's anger may not be directed at a specific individual. Cool down and think of what it is you are angry at and why you are angry. When you do that, you can see what triggered your anger. It was your thinking that "there's absolutely no excuse for something like that." In other words, something happened that was completely opposed to your way of thinking, and caused you to become angry.

In Amida Buddha, the personified symbol of enlightenment, what we call *egoism* does not exist. Amida Buddha does not think of himself as existing in the midst of things and events that are for his free use. In Amida Buddha, there is no trace of hatred or anger, envy or jealousy.

Well, then, does this not mean we should all try to be like Amida Buddha and throw away our egoism, and strive not to harbor thoughts of hatred and anger?

No, that is not what is meant. In our case, as long as we live, due to our having only limited wisdom and virtue, we humans are weak. Strapped with an overabundance of desires, it is only natural that our existence is as it is. We may feel we have been outdone by Amida Buddha as far as goodness, but there is no reason that we should be competing with the Buddha over this.

However, it is important that we recognize hatred and anger as the tricks played upon us by our desires. Do not blame others for your hatred; you must realize that it is born out of your own heart. Once you can do that, when at times that self of yours starts to harbor hatred or anger again, you may notice that a change has come over you.

8

Comfort, the seed of hardship; hardship, the seed of comfort

There's a comedy skit where a father is giving his lazy son a father-to-son talk.

"When you're young, son, you gotta work and endure all kinds of hardships."

Fathers are always worried about their children's futures.

"What's the point of working?" his son retorts.

"Well, son, you work hard, and little by little, you start to enjoy a comfortable life," says the aged father.

"But I'm already enjoying a comfortable life."

What the father means by hardship and comfort, and what the son means by hardship and comfort are two different things, as we can gather from this exchange. The father is saying that if his son works hard and doesn't mind the hardships, then he will be able to live in comfort one day, while the son wants to avoid hardship and thinks only to enjoy a comfortable life every step of the way.

೧೩

The Buddha's work is to rescue those who are suffering. However, the Buddha does not think, "This is something I must do." It is rather a form of enjoyable recreation for the Buddha, with his heart already immersed in the work this requires. Thus, the Buddha is described as literally waltzing through his work carefree; nothing could be more pleasant.

The image that people have of the Buddha varies. There are some who imagine their loved ones and ancestors to be the Buddha, but the term "Buddha" originally meant a person who is awakened. The Buddha who actually existed historically was Shakyamuni.

Shakyamuni was born about 2,500 years ago, as a prince of a kingdom in India. Though it was a small kingdom, as a prince of the country he had status, and if he had chosen, he could have led a life of comfort and enjoyment. However, he gave up his royal status and set out on a journey in which he would have to endure severe ascetic practices.

Why did he abandon the royal life and embark on this arduous journey? Before his awakening, Shakyamuni was, like us, beset by worries and delusions. For the sake of those who are lost in worries and delusions, Shakyamuni explained what he knew in talks that were compiled in a later time, as texts known as sutras. In this sutra literature, Buddhas of all kinds appear, and the stories of how they address the sufferings of the people are manifold. These talks deal with sickness, aging, and death; the sufferings that man cannot evade.

After attaining enlightenment, the Buddha realized that his worries and sufferings shared a common thread with the worries and sufferings of others. Thus, after attaining awakening, he made it his career to relieve the pain and suffering of others.

When he saw people who were worried or suffering, his heart went out to them. That is why it was never a burden for him to go to the rescue of those in suffering. It was sheer recreation for him, something he quite enjoyed doing.

We too, when we do not think of work as torture, can start to enjoy it immensely. Ideally, though, this would mean that we should enjoy what we are doing; not for our own sake or benefit but for the sake and benefit of others.

9

Keep that mirror reflecting your frailty handy

At one event, I met a head minister who told me this story:

The minister's family hardly ever went out for dinner, but one day he took them out to a restaurant.

When their order was served and everyone was ready to eat, his children put their hands together in *gassho*, just like at home and said, "O Buddha, who blesses us with this wonderful meal, it is with deep gratitude that we give our thanks to you for watching over our family."

Everyone in the restaurant turned and stared at them. The young minister felt embarrassed and looked down and hid his folded hands under the table. The children were perplexed and asked, "Papa, why didn't you join us?"

Children are indeed pure at heart. When young people grow up, they become more socially aware. Even someone like the young minister is aware of people watching him and he acts differently.

All of us have been in a situation where we have brushed up against some unseen social convention and unintentionally crossed the line. We are at a loss where to turn in life; adrift in the world, our existence is most fragile. Sometimes we wish we could have the kind of religious convictions of children, but no one can remain a child forever. All of us have to grow up, tossed about by the difficulties of life, to nurture, without having an awareness of ourselves as a part of society.

The reason the minister told us this story was to confess that it was because of this experience, he had an insight into himself. It is through the mirror of the heart that light is cast upon us in all our frailty. This episode made him reflect upon his hypocrisy, thinking, "What I say and what I do are at odds," and that was why he was able to relate this story to us.

❧

In recent times, the news has reported numerous cases of food industry violations where companies have mislabeled goods of which the expiration dates had passed.

As I watched the news, it occurred to me that this was not a case of an especially bad group of people doing their dirty work. This kind of mistake or oversight happens because no one stands up to stop it, and so the problem actually has deeper roots.

Whenever someone announces this kind of scheme to mislabel food packets, there certainly are those who will look into themselves, into the mirror of their hearts, and think, "Why, that's not right, we shouldn't be doing this!" However, when they put priority on the profit to themselves or to the company, that mirror of the heart clouds over. When they become the yardstick to measure these things, they fail to realize the magnitude of their crimes of betraying the trust of the people. From there on out, they begin to sink deeper and deeper into the world of delusion.

When things happen, a brave person, who will steadfastly

stand his ground, will not always be forthcoming. What is important here is to stand back and assess the situation before deciding what to do.

10

Behind our words of sympathy and encouragement, we gloat, how much better off we are!

There is a saying, "When our neighbors move up in the world, our blood pressure goes up too." Similarly, "When our neighbors plant red roses, we grow green with envy." Whenever we compare ourselves to others, we grow jealous of how they are so much better off than we are. We compare ourselves to others even without intending to.

What happens in the reverse case, however, when the person in question is not as fortunate as we are? Do we not hear ourselves heaving a sigh of relief?

On the news, for instance, we see starving children in a war zone who have lost their parents. It is only natural for us to think to ourselves, "Oh, those poor children!" At the same time, in another corner of our mind lurks the thought, "I count myself so lucky that did not happen to me." We are so relieved to be living in a peaceful society. Do we not also experience this kind of feeling of relief?

Again, when we visit a friend in the hospital, we may say some encouraging words like, "Sorry to see you laid up like this, but you'll be better in no time. Hang in there, my friend." Then, in another corner of our mind lurks the thought, "Good thing I am still healthy," or "I am glad that did not happen to someone in my family." Is this not the case?

Seeing someone who is in an unlucky situation, you breathe a sigh of relief, thinking, "Boy, I am much better off than that guy." We may pride ourselves for our honesty and for never telling lies, but this is what we are really like.

However, if we let the mind that is relieved to think, "I am much better off than that guy," grow unchecked, in time it will embrace the arrogant attitude that thinks, "I am somehow special." Such arrogance falls into the danger of nurturing a mentality that discriminates against others, based on the distinction it draws between what is superior and inferior.

CR

Shinran Shonin's heart went out to those who kept comparing themselves to others, who moved back and forth between hope and despair. He sought a path by which even those who had done something wrong or thought themselves to be somehow special could be spiritually saved.

If you never question what you are doing, the process of spiritual rebirth cannot begin. This also goes for self-reflection and inner development, as well as cultivating a true sense of contentment.

The most frightening proposition is that a person can

somehow lose the ability or heart to reflect upon himself.

Always carry that mirror, wherein you can peek into your own heart. In that mirror, you can see reflected thoughts and images long submerged. To do something about the emptiness and hollowness that afflicts you, look into yourself. It is important you see that everything starts from there.

11

Are we losing the art of living, free of calculated effect and attachment to things?

If you look up the word "free" in the dictionary, it says, 1. to do work without receiving any money in return, 2. giving something away and not expecting any money in return; without cost; no charge.

On any given day, our actions inevitably involve some form of calculation. Nothing is free. There is some profit in it for me, and so I make an effort. There is usually no one who would go out of their way to suffer by performing some profitless task.

However, if by some uncalculated action, without any ulterior motive, one were to strive to make someone happy, as well as make oneself happy in the process, how wonderful that would be.

You might wish to make someone else happy, but you want to get some thanks for it, or you want the recipient to be grateful; well, that makes your action calculated. A person who does something without asking, out of a one-sided wish to make someone happy, and quietly goes about working toward that end, putting his entire life into making that wish come true, is called a Buddha.

❧

A few years ago, a television news station showed a photograph of a badly burned cat receiving a transfusion. Suckling at the mother cat was her litter of five kittens. The storage shed of the car repair shop where the kittens were born had caught on fire. The firemen cordoned off the area as they prepared to fight the blaze, but the mother cat skirted past them and ran into the burning shed, bringing out the kittens one by one. Every time she came out, she got singed even more and was growing visibly weaker. Finally, she rescued the last of her litter and collapsed on the spot. The firemen who saw this, once their work was done, took the mother cat to the local veterinary hospital, which managed to save her life. That is the story behind the photograph.

❧

This news item left a big impression on me. The mother cat had done something that even humans rarely do.

In this way, the one who has the will to throw his life into saving the lives of others is a Buddha.

For instance, when Amida Buddha was in the midst of practice, he praised his mentor Lokesvararaja, saying he wanted to become a Buddha of the same caliber.

Even if I should be subjected to
All kinds of suffering and torment,
Continuing my practice undeterred,
I would endure it and never have any regrets.

"Verses in Praise of Buddha," *The Larger Sutra of Infinite Life,* P. 17

In order to come to my rescue, whether the Buddha had to go through fire or water to do so, no matter what excruciating pain the Buddha would have to endure, the Buddha would endure it without regret—*that* is a Buddha.

ଔ

In Buddhism there is the phrase, "the seven gifts that require no possessions." The seven gifts are:

1. The gift of gentle eyes, looking at others kindly.
2. The gift of a smile and kind expressions.
3. The gift of words, speaking kindly to others.
4. The gift of the physical body. Acting properly yourself, and treating others with respect.
5. The gift of heart, touching others with a heart full of love.
6. The gift of a resting place, offering others a place to sit and rest.
7. The gift of shelter and lodging, providing others with a room or warm place to stay.

These seven gifts do not require any money or goods in the least. Of course, we cannot live the way the Buddha did. However, we can emulate the Buddha. When we do so, we can better appreciate what a truly wonderful heart the Buddha must have had in order to accomplish what he did.

Take off your
suit of armor and relax!

The world will look a
whole lot better if you do.

12

Parents do not choose their kids, anymore than kids choose their parents

Once I had a visitor who called on me for some advice about his son. "How old?" I asked.

"35," he said.

Actually, I was inquiring as to the age of the child. My next question was, "How long have you been a father?"

"10 years," he said.

So the child was 10 — and that meant the father was 10. That is, during the 35 years that the man had lived, his life as a father accounted for only the 10 years since his child was born.

A man becomes a parent only from the time his child is born. That is, while this man's actual age amounted to so many years, as for being a parent, his age was always the same number of months and years that his child had lived. "Ah, parent and child are always the same age!" was the thought that occurred to me.

Generally, we tend to think of a parent as having chalked up more knowledge and experience than the child. It is true that an adult may have more knowledge and experience; however, as far as the experience of being a parent is concerned, this is not the case. In fact, it is better to think that with the birth of our child, our life as parents starts from age 0.

Well, then, someone might ask, what if there are two or

more children, what then? In that case, from the birth of the second child, you become a parent of two children for the first time. Likewise, with the birth of your third child, you start all over again as a parent of three for the first time. When you have one child older and one younger, you run into the problem of how to interact with them when raising them. This problem is one that a parent with two or more children confronts for the first time. When a man has a 10-year-old child and a 5-year-old one, his career as a parent spans ten years, but his career as a parent of two children is only five years.

The reason that I have brought this topic up is to say that children are not owned by their parents, and we need to rethink the view, "I am the parent and my kids should do as I say."

അ

It was not a custom of Buddhist origin, but long ago, in Japan, children were not regarded as members of the human world until they had reached the age of 7. The popular *Shichigosan* (7-5-3) ceremony originally had the sense of comforting the family, confirming the children had reached the ages where they would survive and could assume life as human beings.

Only in recent decades has the infant mortality rate in Japan dropped significantly, in part due to the abundance of food and advances in modern medicine. My great grandfather was the sixth child, but by the time he was born, none of the other five brothers and sisters were alive; that was the norm. If a child had the vitality to survive to the age of 7, there was truly a reason to celebrate.

Currently, the infant mortality rate has plummeted, and parents take it for granted that their children will grow well into adulthood.

Not only that, it has now come to the point where parents decide whether or not to give birth to children. I get this strong impression especially when I hear people speaking of "making" children. Since the phrase "to make" implies that it involves the maker's will, this is an unconscious assumption on the part of the speaker. When people talk in this way, they no longer have the sense that they are "blessed" with children, but think of children as their own right to have.

Somewhere along the way, people have gotten on the wrong track, thinking that even their own children should bow to their will.

ؒ

It is natural that parents should have all kinds of dreams and wishes for their children. That said, what about the parents' dream or wish that dictates the outcome of that child's future?

For instance, what if the parents cherish the wish that their child becomes a violinist or baseball player? Even before the child is old enough to understand what he is doing, lessons begin that the child is forced to continue. If the child does not have the talent and interest, there is nothing enjoyable in the lessons. They are sheer torture for the child.

Once I met a boy who complained about this type of situation. He was having a hard time complying with his mother's wishes, to the point he said, "I wish you had never given birth to me." Such was the rage that had built up within him.

It could well be that parents are only thinking about the happiness of their child, but the child is shackled by his parents' wishes and the parent-child relationship suffers as a result.

Children are very sensitive about someone else's ideals being imposed upon them. If what they are being prompted to do simply does not suit them, they think that they still have to go through with it even though they don't like it, and this creates a big conflict in their relationship with their parents.

When you watch children going through the motions just to make their parents happy, as they practice or engage in sports, they don't appear to be happy. On the other hand, if someone's heart is into it, then however hard the practice, that person will not begrudge it.

"Willow green, flower red," means that the willow and the flower are most beautiful when they are radiantly themselves, the willow radiantly green, the flower radiantly red.

Parent and child are mutually the same age. In this sense, the parent-child relationship is just one relationship among the many that people have as human beings. Whatever the reason, it will not do for the parents to unilaterally force their dreams and wishes onto their children.

Just as parents do not choose their children, children do not choose their parents. It is important for parents to have dreams and hopes for their children's future, but when they do not respect the individuality of their children and impose their hopes upon them, such parents are merely assuming that they have the right to dictate their children's lives.

13

There is no one alive who is completely useless

"I haven't done anything, I am just a burden to everyone, I am leading a completely useless life. What a sorry example of a human being I am!"

Someone once told me this.

When you have a chance, take a good, hard look back upon your life. Is there not a twinge of regret or a feeling of remorse that comes trickling up?

I told my guest, "It is a good thing you have such feelings now and then." This person was lucky to have the chance to look back on his life. It was a change for the better, and I told him as much.

However, he turned to me with a rather dour face and said, "No, you see, I don't understand how it is I am supposed to change. It is completely beyond me. The only thing I understand about myself is I am completely useless."

For the time being, you might not have a job, or you might continue to be a burden upon your parents, but that is no reason to belittle yourself by saying that you are a useless person. You are, in this world, a unique existence, and no one can take your place.

When you were born into this world, there was nothing you could do for yourself. Someone had to give you milk, change your diapers, and care for you in order for you to grow. You learned to walk and talk. People around you showed you how to live, and you were brought up showered with wishes for your future. You fell down, got hurt, and became ill at times. You might even have gotten angry and quarreled with others.

There were times that you spent with your parents, siblings, and relatives that have had intangible value for you, which you would not trade for the world. Ah, those cherished memories you have of others! Who can say of themselves that they are completely useless persons?

We do not want to be a burden upon others — that is the honest feeling we all share. The truth is, though, it is not possible to live without being a burden upon others. That is because we all live by mutually supporting one another.

The family is based on each person going to the other person's aid, and at the same time, by each member being a burden upon the others. If, in order to refrain from being a burden upon others, we do not go to anyone for advice and simply decide all things by ourselves, a family would be a very unhappy place. By not seeking the help and advice of others, it would make for disconnected and unsatisfactory relationships. Not consulting others would be cause for even greater concern. Our idea of not wanting to cause trouble may not be identical with what the family considers to be troublesome.

It is laudable for one to become a humble person who looks into oneself, but if you arbitrarily go off the deep end and wallow around in self-pity, all you end up doing is throwing the fine equilibrium of human relationships out of balance.

If you ever feel that what you are doing is putting someone out, it is good to express that honestly in your own way. It is also important to honestly express your thanks to someone who helps you, in light of the understanding that we cannot live without depending upon others.

To the person who told me that he was a useless person, I suggested he express his feelings of thanks honestly to those around him. By directly expressing his feelings of thanks, I expect it will usher in positive changes in his relationships with those around him.

14

The heart realizes its indebtedness to others

Have you ever heard the phrase, "helping each other out with the chores?"

These days, we can do a lot of the farm labor with machines. But, there was a time when anything that had to be done on a farm was a chore that required a lot of hands. When something had to be done, people in the villages and hamlets would all come out and cooperate with one another to help get these chores done.

Whenever there was any work to do on one farm, the neighbors would all come out to help. Of course, everyone did this without payment. In return, when our family needed help, then other people would do the same for us and come to our aid.

If you were a farmer, when it was time to harvest, a rotation was set up and everyone pitched in — today we will harvest the rice at this farm, tomorrow at that farm, and the following day at our farm. This kind of mutual help was not limited to farm work. When a house was in need of a repair, or when a community event was to be held, whether a coming of age day or a wedding, funeral or festival; or when there was construction work to be done, whenever a lot of hands were needed to get some work done, everyone would pitch in to do it.

I helped that family out the other day, so now they owe me, but this kind of accounting did not take place. There was no keeping tabs on lending and borrowing. In bad times there was a feeling that we should mutually help one another out, as many times as was needed.

This act of "returning the favor," as a part of mutually helping each other out, seems to me to be a very natural process.

ଔ

However, with the advent of the capitalist society, these customs were soon abandoned. Whatever work needing to be done now had a price placed on it; everything was based on the concept of buying and selling. In one sense, this made modern life more convenient. The downside was that the feeling of thoughtfulness for others, of helping each other out, has suddenly faded away.

When something other than money is used to mediate the exchange of labor and goods, is there not a kind of warmth to it? That is because there has to be a heart-to-heart exchange between people.

In modern society, the ways in which people interact with one another have undergone rapid changes. The seasonal greetings that were once a unique feature of the Japanese society have been reduced to the stylized greeting cards for New Years and midsummer and year-end gifts.

While such greeting cards are important for maintaining business contacts, are not these greetings more important as a time when we think of how our old acquaintances are doing?

"I wonder how my old friend is doing these days," you think to yourself, as you write a note on a greeting card to him. "It would be nice to send some kind of gift, I suppose." More important than the kind of gift you send is turning your thoughts to that person, and recalling some small things about that person. I think that in itself has significance.

ᗏ

Returning the favor is not limited to those from whom you have directly received a favor. If someone has done something nice to you, it would be wonderful if you returned that feeling of gratitude naturally in quite another setting. If you were to do this for the benefit of those around you, not only would you be pleased by the results, it would also improve your relations with others.

There is a Japanese saying, "When I wanted to do something nice for my parents, it was too late." When you finally come to the age when you want to show your parents how much you really appreciate them, your parents have already passed away, and there are many people in this situation who are filled with regret.

Indeed, it would be better to show your appreciation directly, but it is still not too late. If you take that feeling of gratitude for the kindness they showed when raising you, then direct it to the next generation, this becomes a way of returning the favor to those around you.

Returning the favor is not limited to the world of things. It does not have to be something you *do* for someone else. It is when you have the feeling you want to give something back, when you act out of the feeling that "it was thanks to you that I am what I am." This has the effect of smoothing out your relations with others.

15

Are you starting out each day with a hearty round of good mornings?

"Kids, these days ..."

You only need to hear that much to know what follows will be something negative. The last thing you can expect the speaker to say is something nice about kids.

Although we may ask what is the problem with children today, it is the adults who need to take the blame because of the kind of environment that these children are forced to grow up in.

There are those who persist in blaming the younger generation, passing unfair judgment on them, and saying they are bad. This is most inappropriate. Before criticizing these children, it is the adults who have to first get their acts together.

Let's take a look at how people greet each other.

"Children don't know how to say hello properly anymore."

That is not exactly the case. Indeed, it would be more accurate to say it is the adults who do not know how to greet one another, which has made children incapable of handling greetings properly.

It does seem to be the case since, compared to another day and age, the exchange of daily greetings, such as a good morning, hello, or good night, has become fewer and far between.

It could be that the standard of greetings exchanged

between people, where one greets the other and the other responds in kind, is gradually fading away.

School teachers say that the biggest single factor for this is television's impact on our culture.

Even on television, the announcer starts off with greetings to open the show, saying, "Good morning!" or "Good afternoon!" However, the medium of television is not a means of interactive communication. It is a one-way stream of communication, and as such, it is not possible for the viewers to have an equal exchange. No matter how much we might say our greetings to the screen, or ask questions to it, or seriously answer the questions we are being asked, no mutual conversation takes place.

When people begin to spend hours on end watching television each day, it could well be that they will gradually lose the knack of exchanging greetings with one another and having real give-and-take exchanges.

"Some of the kids, these days ..." one teacher was heard to say.

"During class, some of these kids have a vacant look on their faces. They sit there, looking toward the front, with their mouths open. It occurred to me that these kids are probably the ones who watch television all the time."

There could be a grain of truth in that.

ॐ

In Zen, when Master and disciple engage in a question-answer exchange, this is called a mutual greeting, or *ai-satsu*.

When we look at the origin of this word in the original

Chinese characters, its two elements can be understood as follows: *Ai* 挨 means to open up, to push forward into, to draw near to; and *satsu* 拶 means to press or close in on, to cut into. Taken together the word ai-satsu means to open oneself up, to draw closer to others, to press closer to them, in the process of mutually communicating with one another at a heart to heart level.

My wish would be that, in whatever world we find ourselves, ours might be a society where we can exchange friendly greetings with one another, in a way that conveys warmth and sincerity. It is my hope that the young children, who are to carry on after us, will understand the importance of this exchange between people.

On quite another note, and in what may seem completely contradictory to what I have just said, it is important to teach children that they should never talk to strangers or follow them, because it could lead to serious consequences.

Those who resort to deceive and victimize others are said to be incapable of looking others in the eye; that is, they are unable to greet others. This situation may be a result from people being shut out of their own hearts.

In this sense, it will not do for us to think it makes not the slightest difference whether people heartily greet one another or not. This is something I firmly believe in.

And so, how was it with your family this morning? Was there a hearty round of good mornings exchanged as each of you voiced your greetings?

16

A word of greeting will open the gate surrounding your heart

Out of the blue, the opportunity will sometimes present itself to exchange greetings with someone whom we have never met before.

This happened to me the other day when I went to Tokyo's Kiyosumi Park. The park was featured in a magazine article I had read, and it occurred to me that I would like to see it one day. As I was taking a walk on the pathway around the lake, I happened to strike up a most natural conversation with someone who was a complete stranger to me.

"It is quite beautiful, isn't it?"

"Indeed, it is."

I felt quite elated to have this brief exchange—without any protocol—with someone I had never met before. Of course, some people might say I am making a big to-do over nothing, but this rather unpretentious conversation left me with a brisk, warm feeling.

In this case, we were both entranced by the beautiful scenery surrounding us, and this naturally opened our hearts and made this exchange of greetings possible.

On another occasion some years before, I was taking the *Shinkansen* (bullet train) when it came to an unscheduled stop. It seems that they were experiencing some difficulty with the signal lights further down the track. When we learned this was the case, the person sitting next to me started up a conversation.

"Oh, goodness, what are we going to do?"

"Yes, I wonder when we will be up and running again."

Up to that point, we had not exchanged a single word, and it was likely we would not have had that conversation at all if the train service had not been interrupted. Now, though, we looked each other in the eyes, turned our heads quizzically, and furrowed our brows. That was the kind of conversation we had.

I think this was a kind of mutual greeting, or ai-satsu. Since we were kindred spirits, (as far as both trying to reach our destination as quickly as possible, when the train came to its unscheduled stop) we were suddenly in the same mindset. That was our entire exchange, but it helped to ease the tension of the moment.

One point I would like to make here is that there was no hidden agenda to these words. Words like, "It is beautiful, isn't it?" and "What are we going to do?" and so on, once said, often amount to nothing more than pleasantries we exchange on occasion. In this situation, however, even though the person to whom you are speaking is a complete stranger, when you mutually share the same situation, you both stand on the same plane of thought—this is the beauty of ai-satsu.

Far better than being stuck on a stalled train all by yourself is to have someone who shares the same thoughts with you. After you have looked each other in the eyes and exchanged a few words, somehow you feel much better.

Years ago, there used to be a small café near our temple. The man who ran the place once told me the one thing that really pleased him was when the customers said, *"Go-chiso-sama,"* which was to compliment him on his cooking, as they went out. All he had to hear was that one word. Somehow it made him feel that all the trouble he went through was worth it.

You might say, a word of greeting has the role of gently pushing open the gate surrounding your heart.

Did you ever notice how
the way we live ushers
in a sense of uneasiness
and confusion?

17

Life grows hollow,
not from the tedium of the day,
but from the hardening of the heart

"Everyday I do the same old thing. I can't stand it, it's so boring."

Someone came to me with this complaint.

"How was it when you were a child? When you were going back and forth on the same road to school everyday, was it boring for you then?"

That was the question that I put to my guest.

"No, when I was little, I never thought that way. Around that age, I must have still had some hope for the future. Today, I am just stuck in the rut of a tedious life. Is this how I am going to live out my life, I wonder, doing the same things over and over? I can't tell you how hopeless it feels to be caught in this rut."

From what he told me, I surmised he was locked into a fixed routine.

My guest told me that he had dreams for the future when he was a child. Is this indeed the reason why we do not experience life as empty when we are children?

When I think back on my own childhood, I recall my life as being filled with new discoveries everyday. The way back and forth to school was always the same, but there was always something new to discover. "Today I saw this kind of bird, today I saw a beautiful flower in bloom" — these discoveries I made everywhere I looked. It was the same at school as it was at home. "Someone said this, what does it mean?"—I was full of questions. "What's that fragrance, what's it called?"—I was burning with curiosity. Each and every discovery was unusual and interesting, and I never found myself bored.

A child's view of the world is not bound up by adult values or preconceived notions, and that alone gives the child freedom to see, hear, and feel things.

When we become adults, we become stuck on a certain way of viewing things. "Ah, there's a flower in bloom!" We have that visual input, but then we draw upon our knowledge to determine the name of the flower and to recall the detail of which season it blooms. When we are finished naming the flower and identifying the season, there is nothing in the least interesting left. The best we can do is say, "Oh, look, there is that same old flower blooming again this year." The thrill and surprise of discovery is gone.

When that happens, we are no longer able to feel the sense of freshness and discovery that our situation offers; whether it is a job, meeting someone, seeing something beautiful, or reading a wonderful book. As a result, every day becomes tedious. Is there some way to prevent this from happening?

When you walk down the same road, rather than say to yourself, "Oh, this is the same old road again," you might try to see it from the innocent perspective of the child who asks, "What could there be that's different today?" You will find that the things that enter your field of vision are different. Depending on whether you are riding a car or walking on foot, the things that your eye perceives will naturally be different.

When a small change occurs in what you are doing, and you start to see things in a slightly different way, a different world from what you were ordinarily accustomed to opens up. When that happens, you will find that those nagging thoughts that your everyday life is tedious and boring have disappeared.

Isn't the cause for the hollowness of your life due, not to your life per se, but to the way you are pursuing it?

CR

In the language of *Chanoyu*, or Tea Ceremony, there is a saying, *"Ichigo, ichie,"* which means the tea ceremony is a once in a lifetime event. When this ceremony is arranged, you must do it as a unique event that all of your guests will enjoy, with nothing wanting in the least. It may well be that some of your guests will be attending three days running, but one must never regale them with the same stories as on the previous day, nor embrace your guests with the feeling that you have just entertained them the day before. Whatever you do, this time, this moment will never come around again.

Rennyo Shonin (1415-1499) the 8th Monshu of our Hongwanji, left us these words:

> In the way of Buddha, there is no talk of tomorrow
>
> *— Rennyo Shonin Goichidaiki kikigaki*

And further he says,

It is as if you were hearing something for the first time and you were to let it always remain something rare and wonderful, as if hearing it for the first time — that is how it is when you are in the state of faith. You might imagine it as always wanting to be in a state of hearing something rare and wonderful. No matter how many times you hear that one thing, it is so rare and wonderful it is as if you were hearing it for the first time.

— *Goichidaiki kikigaki*, P. 130

Rennyo Shonin is saying when a person follows the way of the Buddha, it is not possible to say, "Let's do this tomorrow," for in that pursuit, no matter how many times you may have heard the same talk, what you are hearing *now*, you listen to as if hearing it for the first time.

When one listens to talks on Buddha, this is called *chomon*, or "listening with the ears of the heart." On the wall of one temple, there is a sign that says, "How to listen with the heart:"

1. You should listen as if you are listening for the very first time.
2. You should listen as if the message is for you alone.
3. You should listen as if this is the last time you will ever do so in your life.

When you let these words become etched into your heart, I think you will one day find you are no longer sighing over "Oh, how boring" each day is.

18

So tell me, what is reflected in that mirror of yours?

The poet Shosaku Asada has a poem titled, "Mirror," which says:

> *Every morning, every morning,*
> *I would face that mirror over the sink.*
> *What did I think I was looking at,*
> *I wonder.*

There are not many people who get up in the morning and go out without looking in the mirror. As we wash up, brush our teeth, and get ready to go out, we look in the mirror time and time again. This is something we repeat every day.

Then one day, out of the blue, you quietly ask yourself, "What am I looking at every morning when I look in the mirror?" Then it occurs to you that, when you see yourself reflected in the mirror, you are seeing only your outward form. The person who you are is someone who is seen by others, and so you peek in the mirror to check whether there is something odd or not quite right with your appearance.

If you were living on an uninhabited island, you might go through your daily routine not looking in the mirror at all.

How we appear to others is not just a matter of outward appearance.

We are also concerned about what people think of us. Is

what we are doing sanctioned by society? If we do this, will we become the object of ridicule by those around us? More than that, we wonder what people will think of us, as people. This is something we cannot simply ignore. Here, in the absence of some absolute rule by which we judge ourselves, we constantly evaluate ourselves by the way others judge us.

Further, when it comes to our actual performance at school or at work, of course we are concerned about our status in relation to other people. Test results or monthly quotas, where people are lined up by rank, become the critical standard for evaluating ourselves. "My grades aren't outstanding, but I am satisfied with them because I tried my best."—It would be great if we could think that way, but it just doesn't work out like that. We keep comparing ourselves to others, and end up asking ourselves, was my score better than average? Did I get a better grade than the next person?

When you get a better than average grade on your test, you feel relieved. If you have a better than average income, then you feel you are living a cut above the middle. We even look at the average life span as a standard for how long we want to live. We have become so accustomed to measuring ourselves by the average value that when we evaluate ourselves as human beings, we decide on the basis of the average.

Everyone, as human beings, lives with a wish for their lives. This wish becomes our basic driving force. In the course of our drive to achieve the goals we set for ourselves, it becomes our reason to live—and this, I think, is most significant.

However, when this wish turns out to be a wish to live in a bigger house, or a wish for more money, or a wish for higher status, or a wish for more power, then a person tumbles into the pit of unbridled greed. When it becomes a wish to subjugate others, or a means to look down on others, this is far from the trajectory set by our original wish and can only be called its degenerate form.

To whatever heights you may climb in your career, however much power you may gain, within each of us is a person who does not want to lose sight of himself. I think that person within is reflected in the mirror of your heart.

19

Everyone grows old, that's just part of our mission in life

"There's nothing more important than your health."

"You can say that again. Health is everything."

I am sure everyone has had this kind of conversation at one time or another.

In recent years, there has been an unprecedented boom in the health and lifestyle industry, with products touted as "good for you" enjoying great popularity. When a new product is advertised on television to be "good for health" or having some health benefit, the next day everyone flocks to the store in droves to buy it and the item soon vanishes off the shelves.

Why do people wish to be so healthy? I would contend this high interest in health is being fueled unconsciously by a strong fear of growing old and falling ill.

Compared to the past, people today have much greater access to information about personal health and illness. If a person is suffering from a malady of some kind, then takes the "best" method of treatment, consequently he will be cured much sooner than if he had taken something else. There are also various preventative measures, which we are told can achieve the same ends. What if we happen to miss out on one, though— well, that may well seal our fate! It is this uncertainty that has people jumping out of their seats and running to the store every time they hear some new bit of information.

When we imagine ourselves being stricken with illness and our bodies growing old, we are frozen with fear. The uncertainty of this situation is so gripping that we wish to do everything to prevent it from happening. And it is altogether natural that we think this way. No matter how careful we are with our health, though, it is impossible to avoid sickness and injury, nor can anyone escape growing old and feeble.

To take measures to protect one's health and to be concerned about one's physical condition is not necessarily bad. On the other hand, when you take care of your health out of a wish to always be healthy, you will become consumed by the idea and lose perspective on what lies ahead.

However much one may try to prevent it, all people grow

old. You cannot turn your eyes away from that truth. In other words, it is important to map out a strategy to welcome old age into your life. Once your heart is prepared for the change, the hard edge is taken off your feelings of uncertainty with regard to growing old.

You do not have to feel embarrassed about growing old, nor should you think it distasteful to do so. For me, growing old is the last item on the agenda left to do. I think of it as the final mission that I must see to. As we let the years pile upon us, we should regard this as part of the work we are being called on to do. It is the honest role that we are being called upon to play in the drama of life.

ॐ

My father passed away in June of last year. He was 90 years old.

When I saw my aged father lying in this state, I remembered how moved I was by the passage from the *Tannisho*:

> However hard it may be to bid farewell to this world, when the conditions that bind us to this *saha* [samsara] realm run out, we are powerless to do anything as the final hour arrives and we are swept away to that Land.
>
> — *A Record in Lament of Divergences,*
> *The Collected Works of Shinran (CWS), Vol. 1,* P. 666

I was particularly struck by this passage because my father lived to such an advanced age. However fortunate the circumstances in his old age, as the years advanced, things became harder for him to do and he grew weary. The final six months he was hospitalized, we had to leave the care for his daily needs entirely in the hands of the staff attending to him.

We generally think if people live long lives, how lucky they are. But seeing my father become old and feeble, I let my thoughts, again, dwell deeply on the problem of old age.

As a result, I thought long and hard on the matter of how I myself should enter old age, and how my immediate family should be affected by it. In other words, it was through seeing the example of how my aged father lived out his old age that I began to think seriously and concretely about my own old age and death.

How a person lives out his old age, as well as how a person dies, are things that one wishes to have others think about, beginning with your children and grandchildren. Is this not the final task that we are obliged to carry out?

"As long as you live, it is your fate as a human being to grow old. Though you are now young, in the future you must face the problem of living out your old age. Learn from watching the way I have been living, this is my solution to that problem."

That is what a grandparent might say to his children and grandchildren. There is never anyone who is completely useless in this world or whose life is without meaning. Achieving old age is noble and to be respected — yours is an important role that you have been assigned, to convey this message to others.

Recently, it seems there has been an increasing number of people who do not want to show others that they have grown old and frail. They do not want to show others how old and unsightly they have become. Although they may think this way, in fact, there is nothing unsightly about old age.

"Before I used to be able to do this with no trouble, but now I cannot adequately take care of the things that pertain to my own life." This is the complaint we sometimes hear people say.

Of course, it is hard for us to think we cannot get around as easily as we once did anymore. "I have to ask people to help me, and there is nothing I can do in return. Oh, I am just a big burden on others." This is the way we end up thinking.

However, everyone has to grow old sometime. Whether you are elderly or young or in your infancy, all of us live by depending upon one another.

Our life is not our possession. It is through the support of numerous other lives that we manage to live. Amongst the numerous links that exist, one of the living links is this: our life.

"Now that I have grown old, I am a burden to those around me." When you get deadlocked into that kind of thinking, this generates your uncertainty and pain over growing old. When you accept this is how you ought to appear and start to think that it is your personal mission to look as you do, you will feel much better.

"Ours is to grow old" is an important message and it is our important role to bring this message to the attention of future generations.

When you accept who you are and openly receive the help of others, it is possible to say from the heart such words of appreciation as, "thank you so much." When I notice that there is someone who will look after me and take care of me when I am old and sick, I feel most appreciative and joyful. If it is within the realm of possibility, is that not where you want to be, too?

ભ

Before Shakyamuni renounced worldly life, as the prince of a small kingdom in India, he lived a carefree life.

One day, just as he was going out through one of the castle gates, he met an elderly man and was awakened to the reality of old age. Later, he recalled this moment and said:

> Again, monks, I thought: One of the uneducated common folk ... when he sees another person subject to death ... is disgusted and ashamed, forgetful that he himself is such a one. Now I too am subject to death. I have not passed beyond death, I might be troubled ...That would not be seemly in me. Thus, monks, as I considered the matter, all pride in my life deserted me.

> —"Delicately Nurtured," Anguttara Nikaya III. 4.38; Woodward Tr.

Seeing the feeble old man and realizing that he, too, would become like him, first Shakyamuni rejected the idea, thinking, "I do not want to become like that—how miserable!" Then, thinking again, he was able to accept that he, too, would naturally grow old. He was able to single out this insight into suffering, that old age surely visits us all. He had direct insight into this truth that no one can evade.

In Buddhism, birth, old age, sickness, and death are the four basic forms of suffering for people. When Shakyamuni saw that these four sufferings rooted in existence were the ones we all had to inevitably endure, he found in them a starting point.

When a person takes on this last assignment as a human being, that is, "growing old," something opens up to that person. A person arrives at something completely apart from his usual preoccupation with social status and the business of life. By working through the various scenarios of growing old, a person thus awakens to ultimate truth. It is there we begin to see the meaning of growing old.

20

Where do you suppose you came from?

In times past, after the harvest had been brought in and no farm work could be done, people who lived in farming villages would spend a few days during the winter season at one of the hot springs to rest and recuperate.

Cheerfully chatting amongst themselves, they would soak leisurely in the hot springs. The winter season was the only chance they had to pass the time this way. And so, when they did, they tended to enjoy the good life.

During this season, there was almost surely to be a resident priest on hand. This was in order to let the visitors of the hot springs hear Buddhist messages. Unlike today, this was a time when there were not many amusements. The priest's talks would not be difficult moral discourses admonishing the audience, but lighter talks that were easier to relate to. For the farmers in the audience who were ordinarily too busy with farm work to visit the temple, listening to these sermons was also a form of entertainment.

Freed from their busy daily schedule on the farms to relax at the hot springs, where they were able to listen to various kinds of Buddhist talks, people had a chance to think about the path to salvation. This allowed them to become refreshed in body and mind.

Taking a hint from their example, it might be good for us to enjoy the good life by being idle for a while.

These days, if there is a time when we are idle, we tend to become alarmed for some reason. It may be impossible for us to take extended time off, but when we notice ourselves getting busy, it might be well for us to stop, and take a few minutes to be idle. By doing that, not only can we see ourselves more objectively, I think we would also tend to be more tolerant of others.

Oh, Mr. Waterbug!
You're forever making circles in the pond in your square-foot world.
From whence do you come?
To whither do you journey?

Hey, pal, bug off, can't ya see I'm busy!

This is a poem called "Mr. Waterbug," by the poet Shijimi Murakami. It is unique because there is a gap between the first few lines and the last line, which leaves a deep impression on us. We say that we are busy, as we pass each day running around in circles, but seen from the eyes of the Buddha, it is no different than the waterbug making circles in its little world. The square-foot world refers to a square-foot space where the waterbug is getting worked up as it's running around.

"Where did I come from, where am I going? Why was I born, why have I grown tall, why must I die?" These questions flit across everyone's minds at one time or another. Answering them, however, is by no means simple. When it is too much to handle, we think, "I don't have time to think about it, and if I had the time, wouldn't it be better for me to get more work done instead?" And so should we accept that for an answer? And that is how we pass the days of our lives. This portrait of man is illustrated in the last line of the poem like a blot of ink. However busy we might be, ours is just an existence caught up in a square-foot world.

CR

Rennyo Shonin, who is regarded as the great revitalizer of Jodo Shinshu, composed a letter called, "On the White Ashes,"

> *Though in the morning we may have radiant health,*
> *In the evening we may be white ashes.*
>
> Taitetsu Unno Tr.

In the morning, we start off the day most vigorously, but by evening, we might well be dead and reduced to ashes. This is a sentiment relating the transiency of life to us.

When you contemplate this poem, it reminds you to reflect upon yourself, no matter how busy you are. In your daily life, it is especially important to take time to answer, "From whence did you come, to whither do you journey?" This is a question that one must ask oneself, and in order to do so, we need to make the room in our busy schedules to think about it at length.

21

Are you listening carefully to that important voice within?

I have spoken about how important it is to have times you spend doing nothing. There is another thing I would recommend, and that is to sharpen the senses.

For instance, you might try sharpening your ears.

Close your eyes, and concentrate only on the sounds that come into your ears, and you will hear sounds you never noticed when your eyes were open. The voices of birds singing, the chirping of insects, the sound of wind—all of the things in the world around us, which we ordinarily would not notice in our daily lives, we can now hear.

Once, when everyone else had gone to sleep and it was quiet, I remember being startled by the croaking of frogs. I wondered how many frogs were out there, I remember thinking, the chorus of their booming voices leaving its low note tingling in my ear. Of course, it is not only at that hour when the frogs croak. They could well be croaking all day and night, but the only time it reaches my ear is always late at night.

Due to all the noise people make, we cannot hear the frogs croaking at any other time. That is, the frogs are probably croaking all of the time, but usually we unconsciously filter out the voices of frogs.

Each of our five senses is extremely sensitive. However, in the course of an ordinary day, we do not put our faculties to full use. We perceive something through a total sensory experience — its appearance, its smell, its sound, its touch, and so on. Above all, I think we are especially prone to being influenced by the information that we perceive through our eyes.

And so, in the hustle and bustle of life, in order to sharpen our senses of half-forgotten sounds and sights, as well as colors and fragrances, it is important that we occasionally suspend our usual use of our five senses. We consciously give each of these faculties a break, by immersing ourselves in the exercise of sensing things, say, through our ears alone.

০৪

On another note, let's think about how this pertains to your life.

You want to ask something of someone. It doesn't matter if it is a personal matter or something related to work, such as a contract. You are not sure, though, if that person will listen to you or not, and you are a bit concerned about it. Just at that time, someone else comes to you with some other kind of matter to discuss. Are you capable of earnestly paying attention to the problem being brought to you?

At any other time, you might make a good listener. Today, though, this business of asking someone about some matter consumes your attention, and you really are not in any mood to listen.

Is this situation not similar to the voices of frogs croaking that we should be able to hear but do not? When we are filled with our own worries, the voices of others can barely enter our ears. This is because we are too preoccupied to listen.

At such times, stop right there, close your eyes, and open the ears of your heart. When you can sharpen the ears of the heart, things you ordinarily would not hear can be heard, and you can now pay attention to the person who has something to ask of you.

The voice of the Buddha is the same as this.

When you go to the gods and buddhas and pray to them with a heart filled with your own wishes and desires, your head is so filled with the things you wish to ask that it is impossible for you to hear the voices of others; in this case, the voice of the Buddha. In order to hear the voice of the Buddha calling you, it is important you strain the ears of the heart to catch the sounds that you usually do not hear. By doing so, you are able to hear the wish that the Buddha places on you, and the world opens up. This experience is what Jodo Shinshu calls, "listening with the ears of the heart."

If you are a person who is more inclined to talk rather than listen to others, you might make a conscious effort to turn an ear to the conversations of others. New horizons could open up for you.

22

Faith is not a matter of pleading for the gods and buddhas to intervene on your behalf

If you put your mind to it, you can do it;
If you do not, you cannot — that is true for all things.
When something cannot be done, you are the one to blame
For not putting your heart into it.

— Yozan Uesugi

This poem conveys the message of Yozan Uesugi, Lord of the Yonezawa clan, who restored the fortunes of the clan to his vassals. You can do it if you try — this is a well-known message, urging people to make an all-out effort.

In the face of the problems generated by this world, it is important that we make a wholehearted effort toward solving them. However, when it comes to real problems, if we ask whether our efforts will be rewarded or whether we will be the happier for it, the answer is that is not always the case. There are some problems with which we can make headway. But, there are other problems for which there is simply no solution forthcoming — that is the reality of human life.

In a sense, the questions of why was I born, for what reason am I living, and why must I die, are among those that defy answers.

Well, if it makes no difference whether we make an effort to solve these questions or not, what should we do? What must we do to attain happiness? The person who thought about these problems and discovered an answer is Shakyamuni Buddha.

ଔ

Someone once told me, "I am a person who is put off by the word 'religion' for some reason. Whenever there is something beyond our power to achieve, we go running to the gods and buddhas to plead their intervention. That is the impression I have of religion."

I told that person the following story:

Once there was a solitary traveler, who had lost his way in the dark woods. However, he had confidence in his own abilities. And so, without the slightest twinge of fear or anxiety, he decided he would continue to walk as long as there was daylight. "No matter how wide the forest, it could not go on endlessly," he thought. "If I keep on walking without taking a break, surely I will leave the forest behind." He was so sure he could do it that he earnestly set out walking without stopping.

However, after several days of walking, he was still lost in the woods, which seemed to continue on endlessly. The man had become so weary that he stopped and took a look around himself. When he looked carefully, he realized this was the very place where he first had noticed he was lost. Day after day, he had walked without stopping, only to arrive at the place where he had started. When he noticed this, all the strength went out of him and he sat down.

When he heard the ominous rustling of the trees and the howling of the creatures of the woods, the man who once had so much confidence in himself began to grow uneasy and cringe with fear. In the man's mind, the fear that he would never leave the forest behind, no matter how much he walked, began to impose itself. At the same time, he looked around himself anxiously, and was so filled with fear that he could no longer move.

In a different part of the woods, another traveler had also become lost. This man first sat down to think about what to do. Turning his face toward the night sky, he saw a star that he could use as a guide. Depending upon that star, he began to walk in a certain direction. When he was uncertain as to the direction to take, he waited until night fell and the star appeared. Once he saw the star, he could verify where he was. Little by little, he was able to walk in one set direction.

The ominous sounds of the forest and the howling of beasts did not make him anxious in the least. In the mind of this person, there was always a shining star to guide him, and there was no reason for him to worry.

In the case of the latter person, he was not pleading for the star to intervene on his behalf. There was nothing that the star was doing directly for the sake of the man. However, the star shone upon that man, and he used its light to guide his path as he continued to walk along.

Isn't this what is meant by entrusting in Buddha?

23

Other Power does not mean counting on other people

Other Power is none other than the power of Tathagata's Primal Vow.
— *The Collected Works of Shinran (CWS)* P. 57

This is what Shinran Shonin states, that Other Power is the working of Amida Buddha.

The term "Other Power" was originally used by the Chinese monk Tan-luan, more than 1,500 years ago.

Shinran Shonin attached great importance to this term, and realizing its importance, he naturally gave it a central role in his teachings.

Buddhist literature abounds with unique phrases and expressions, but there is, perhaps, no single phrase that has continued to be more misunderstood than "the Vow of Other Power." Often, the phrase is understood to mean, "I do not have to do a thing. I can depend completely on everyone else," or "I can count on others," but actually this is far from its original meaning.

In the past, Buddhism was thought to teach that if a person piled up effort, it was possible for the person to become a buddha. Shinran Shonin also followed such thinking, and did practices to that end on Mount Hiei for a period of 20 years. By the time the 9-year-old boy who ascended Mount Hiei became the 29-year-old Shinran Shonin, he met Honen Shonin. Honen Shonin's teaching overturned the conventional Buddhist thinking he had held up to then. It was not that a person piled up efforts to become a buddha, it was rather a wish coming from the Buddha toward man, which asked, "How can I make a buddha out of you?"—Shinran Shonin believed this was true Buddhism.

This, then, is the Vow, or wish, of the Buddha.

In Buddhism, there are many buddhas. A buddha is a being who makes a wish or vow and then carries it out, with each of the various buddhas making their own individual vows. Amida Buddha established his own unique set of 48 Vows. The 18th of those vows is one in which the Buddha vows to save all living things. This is known as Amida's Primal Vow. It is also called the "solemn oath." In Indic languages, the word "oath" originally contained the sense of having made a decision and expressed a strong determination, which indicated, "I shall surely bring it to pass."

When I stand on the verge of buddhahood, there will be
sentient beings in every direction who will, with sincerity
and joy, express a desire to be born in my Land, even as few
as ten times. If they are not born there, may I not receive the
highest Enlightenment.

— "Vow 18," *The Sutra of Infinite Life*

This passage means Amida Buddha is saying, "When I become
a buddha, people everywhere will, with believing hearts, wish
to be born in my Land, though saying the Nembutsu as few as
ten times, and if they are not born, may I never proceed on-
ward to enlightenment." Amida Buddha is saying, "I cannot
stand to leave my Vow unfulfilled. Know for a fact that I will
come to your rescue!" This is the Buddha's deepest wish.

As you will recall, we started this essay with a quotation by
Shinran Shonin, that "Other Power is none other than the
power of Tathagata's Primal Vow," where Other Power equals
the working of Amida Buddha. Have you now arrived at an
understanding of this point? When Shinran Shonin speaks of
his being saved through the power of Amida's Vow and his being born into the Pure Land, it is being brought about by the
working of the Vow of Other Power.

As such, the Vow of Other Power does not mean you're
counting on other people. Nor does it mean putting something
in the offertory box with the expectation of gaining something for yourself. There is no granting of wishes to benefit
you as an individual. The Buddha does not work to make
the wishes of man come true. The Vow of Other Power works,

rather, to let us hear the wish the Buddha places in us.

24

There is more to your legacy than fame, fortune, and family

Man seeks fame, fortune, and power. Behind this is the strong desire to assert the proof of his existence, "I am here, I am alive." Is this not the case?

As proof of your existence, you want to have something to show for a lifetime of effort. When you think of it, things like fortune and power are extremely convincing ways to indicate that.

Another proof of your existence is in the living ties to the next generation, your children and grandchildren.

However, the absence of such things does not mean you do not have living proof of yourself. One person who lost everything — his fame, his fortune, the child whom he trusted — yet strode his path in life was Shinran Shonin.

☙

Shinran Shonin was born in Kyoto and ordained at the age of 9. After that, he lived a life of Buddhist practice for 20 years on Mount Hiei. During that time, the basics of Buddhism became second nature to him.

In those days, Buddhism in Japan was built around the

model of the saintly practitioner who, through his own practice, was able to sever his blind passions and achieve awakening.
However, Shinran Shonin turned toward the Pure Land path,
where, through the working of Amida Buddha, a person seeks
to be born into the Pure Land. Leaving Mount Hiei, he heard
the teaching of Honen Shonin, who taught that it was through
the Nembutsu that we are born in the Pure Land. For this reason, the traditional form of Buddhism was turned around
completely and a new form developed.

Shinran Shonin was subjected to persecution by the author-
ities and exiled to distant Echigo. He was stripped of his official
status as a priest, but Shinran Shonin was not concerned about
such titles, and continued to walk the path of a Buddhist. Living
together with the ordinary people who lived by the sweat of
their brows, Shinran Shonin sought a form of Buddhism all
people could believe in.

At last, his sentence of exile was officially lifted. The ordinary person who had been exiled would want to return to
the old capital of Kyoto, to resume his life. Shinran Shonin,
however, chose not to return to Kyoto. Instead, he turned his
attention to spreading Buddhism in the Kanto (Tokyo) area,
where it had yet to be firmly cultivated.

This was during the period when the government was lo-
cated in Kamakura. The Kanto area lay at the doorstep of the
government center and was a region that was just emerging
as a new center of political power. Whereas the Nembutsu
teaching might have been regarded as radical in Kyoto, where

old traditions continued to be cultivated, Shinran Shonin might have thought the same teaching could have a chance in this newly emerging region.

In this way, he promoted Buddhism from his 40s to his 60s, mainly in the present-day Ibaraki and Tochigi prefectures.

Shinran Shonin married a woman by the name of Eshinni. These days, it is common for a priest to marry, but in those days it was unthinkable. The situation was such that no one would even listen to what a married clergyman had to say. Heading to an area he had never seen before and knew nothing about, he no doubt had to endure unimaginable sufferings to spread the teachings.

Shinran Shonin was the type of person who, even if he ran into a wall, would proceed to pick himself up and positively seek a new approach. Throughout the events that marked the various chapters of his life, as well as his day-to-day life, he broadened and deepened his understanding of the teaching of the Nembutsu, to establish a Buddhism that would welcome all people.

Eventually, Shinran Shonin returned to Kyoto. He did not have his own house and only took up temporary residence there. When the place he was staying burned down, he was forced to move into the temple of a disciple. In his final years, he had no place of his own. In these circumstances, he managed to pursue a literary life, composing letters and religious verses.

Shinran Shonin had a son named Zenran, his eldest, whom

he entrusted with the role of spreading the teachings in the Kanto area. However, when it became clear Zenran's preaching was substantially different from what Shinran Shonin taught, he was forced to disown Zenran. For Shinran Shonin, being true to the teachings, which he spent his whole life spreading, was that important.

In that day and age, it was amazing for a person to live into their 80s. It was after Shinran Shonin was in his mid-80s that he energetically began to produce his writings. The bulk of his literary work dates to these final years. In this way he lived, unattached to home or property, passing away at the age of 90.

☙

We may well ask why we should be drawn to Shinran Shonin.

One reason is, in a life full of hardship and suffering, he strove with all his might, walking the path he knew to be his life without giving up. That image of Shinran Shonin gives us courage.

"Although the world finds it difficult to accept the way I believe, I did not abandon that way of thinking and give in to the demands of the world."—We can sense this strong sense of purpose in Shinran Shonin. He was convinced that, more than the Buddhist model of monastic practice to achieve satori, it was more important for him to establish a path that opened up the way of enlightenment to all people. Here, we can sense the gentleness of manner of someone who had personally undergone a spiritual transformation that had affected a dramatic change to his world.

Also, Shinran did not choose to live the life of a monastic, as he had a wife and children. The fact that he had to disown his own son points to an all-too-human life, full of the sufferings and misgivings that all of us experience at one time or another.

It is for this very reason the words of Shinran Shonin, being drawn from real life, hold an attraction for us and have the power to resonate within us.

Shinran Shonin sought to take the teaching of his mentor Honen Shonin and develop it theoretically, to give it a broader and deeper literary and doctrinal appeal. We might say, Shinran Shonin sought to take up the mission that Honen Shonin could not complete within the space of his lifetime and, out of indebtedness to his mentor, felt compelled to continue the task and bring it to completion.

I think the great attraction of Shinran Shonin lies in the fact that he pursued his own way of life. He was unaffected by what the world thought of him, not letting it pass final judgment on him, not letting himself be swept away by changing circumstances, in order to live a life underscored by his religious convictions.

25

On what should we base our actions for living?

Shinran Shonin held Prince Shotoku (Shotoku Taishi 574-621) in such high esteem that he praised him as the Shakyamuni of Japan.

When we speak of Prince Shotoku, his name is associated with that of his aunt, Empress Suiko Tenno, under whose reign capable men were sent out throughout the country and abroad, to lay down the foundations for a new country.

The Prince was only 49 years old when he died. After he died, his wife Tachibana no Ohiratsume commissioned two embroidered scrolls on which were depicted the Buddha-land to which the prince had gone. These were called the Scrolls of the Land of Heavenly Life, one of which still remains.

When Suiko Tenno saw them, Tachibana no Ohiratsume told her:

> Our great Lord told us, this world is vain and false, only the
> Buddha alone is true.

As the original Japanese is rather difficult to understand, elaboration is needed:

> When our great Lord was alive, there was a saying of which
> he was most fond. For man, there is nothing in this world
> that man has created that can be said to be ultimately real.

The only exception is the Buddha. The Buddha alone is ultimately real.

When Suiko Tenno heard this, she ordered several of her attendants to embroider copies of these two scrolls.

Here, the words, "The world is vain and false" appear on those two scrolls. We can find the same sentiment expressed in Article Ten of Prince Shotoku's *Seventeen Article Constitution.*

> Let the rage in your heart subside, put away your angry looks, do not grow indignant over your differences with others. People all have hearts, and hearts are bound to have their preferences. What they are inclined to like is the very thing we reject, and what we are inclined to like is the very thing they reject. Just as surely as we are not sages ourselves, we can be just as sure that they are not all fools, the both of us being merely ordinary mortals.
>
> *— Seventeen Article Constitution*

Let your indignation subside, put your anger aside, it will not do to fume when others do not do what you say. All people each have their own minds, and each mind is caught up in its own thoughts. That person is not us anymore than we are that person. Just as we are not always wise, others are not always foolish.

We all have our own minds, and that mind has a self-centered way of seeing things and supports a self-centered way of thinking. For that reason, a person always thinks in terms of what is or is not convenient to himself, what is of loss or gain to himself, and what is useful or useless to himself. Seeing others as friend or foe, he lets himself decide what is good or evil, right or wrong—this is man. Under a veneer of plausible explanation, he seeks to present himself as being in the right.

However, there is nothing more dangerous than this kind of mind. This mind is always trembling with lust and hate, and drawing a line between friend and foe. If nothing is done to curb it, it will leave the world ravaged by wars, time and again.

This being the case, whichever person we are speaking of, there is never a person who has not committed some kind of wrongdoing; it is not possible for human beings to be perfect. Further, it is not always the case that the other person was wrong, or the other person had made a mistake. Never think you alone are right. It is better to have good insight into the fact that we mutually live at the mercy of our self-attachment and selfish desires, which spin us about at will, and we are all struck from the same basic mold of unenlightened beings.

From his insight into the fact that, "both of us are merely ordinary mortals," Prince Shotoku arrives at the conclusion: "this world,"—himself included—"is vain and false."

If we next ask what the unenlightened person should use as a guideline for his actions, an answer can be found in Article Two of the *Seventeen Article Constitution*.

> Sincerely revere the Three Treasures. The Three Treasures are: Buddha, Dharma, and Sangha. This is the homeland to which all four walks of life return, this is the highest ideal by which all countries should be governed. There is no age in

which people cannot find this Dharma to be noble. Those who are extremely wicked are few, but when they are taught the Dharma, they can follow it. Unless they align themselves with the Three Treasures, on what basis can they correct their mistaken ways?

— Seventeen Article Constitution

Here, Prince Shotoku says we should revere the Three Treasures from our hearts.

To restate this passage:

The Three Treasures are the Buddha, his teaching, and the community that gathers to listen and live by the teachings of the Buddha. To live and let live is, in the final analysis, the highest form of religion for any nation. No matter the era or person, there is none who does not respect the Buddhist teachings. The wicked among men are not many. If properly taught, they can learn to follow the teachings. Short of taking shelter in Buddhism, how else can their twisted minds be made straight?

"If neither the world nor I have any ultimate truth to speak of, well then, I should just live it up while I can." If you take that attitude, you will end up living a shallow life. This is not what is meant here. For a person who sees the falseness of his life, "to truly live" in this world where nothing is true, means to realize the life of one who turns to the awakened one (Buddha), that is ultimately real. It is to depend on the teachings (Dharma) of the Buddha, and to put oneself in the community (Sangha) of those who seek to live by the teachings of the Buddha. The person who realized this ideal in political terms was Prince Shotoku.

In the *Tannisho* are the words:

> But with a foolish being full of blind passions, in the fleeting world—this burning house—all matters without exception are empty and false, totally without truth and sincerity. The Nembutsu alone is real.
>
> — *The Collected Works of Shinran (CWS)*, P. 679

People like us are ordinary unenlightened people, who are afflicted with blind passions of every kind. This world is like a house on fire in which we run about frantically. Everything in this world is vain and false. There is nothing that can be called real. Inside that world, the only thing that can be said to be true is the Nembutsu. These are the thoughts of Shinran Shonin.

Some 600 years passed between the time of Prince Shotoku and Shinran Shonin. At the same time, the words of the *Tannisho* capture and transmit the spirit of Prince Shotoku.

**Though in the morning
we may have radiant health,
in the evening
we may be white ashes**

—Rennyo Shonin (Taitetsu Unno Tr.)

26

We are born alone and we die alone

Though a person may be the center of love and affection whilst in this world, man is born alone and dies alone, departs alone and arrives alone. Pending the karma he activates, he is set to arrive at either a realm of suffering or a realm of joy. The journey that awaits is one only he can make; no one else can take his place.

— *The Larger Sutra of Infinite Life*, P. 31

When the time comes for us to be born into this world, we are born alone. When the time comes for us to depart, we depart alone. This is the reality for each of us. No matter how many friends may surround us, there is no one who can take our place. We go alone when the time comes.

How, then, can we live, in light of the sheer demand life places on us? But, this is where our inquiry into Buddhism begins.

ଔ

In the time of Shakyamuni Buddha, there lived a young girl named Kisa Gotami, who lived in the city of Savatthi in India.

Kisa married a rich man with whom she had a child. Tragically, just when the child was beginning to walk, the child fell ill and died.

Stunned and in grief, Kisa was unwilling to believe her child had died. She held the cold, lifeless body next to her and ran out into the streets, pleading with whomever she met, "Please, good sir, please cure my child's illness."

One of Shakyamuni's followers witnessed the scene, and calling to Kisa, told her, "Indeed, your child is gravely ill. There is nothing an ordinary doctor can do. However, there is one person who can do something to cure your child's illness. That is Shakyamuni, who is now residing at Jetavana Vihara. You must call upon him."

Kisa immediately went to see Shakyamuni at Jetavana Vihara, saying to him, "Please, save my child!"

Shakyamuni quietly listened to all Kisa had to say, then he gently said, "To cure your child's illness, you must bring some mustard seeds to me, five or six will do. Go now and bring them back to me right away."

Kisa arose from where she was seated and was about to set off. Just at that point, Shakyamuni said to her, "However, those mustard seeds must come from a house where death has never once occurred."

Without fully understanding the Buddha's last words, Kisa left, unable to think about anything else other than saving the life of her child. She hurried into town and went from one house to another, asking for some mustard seeds.

Everyone kindly gave her some mustard seeds. However, when she asked the family whether this was a house where death had never once occurred, there was no home that had never experienced death.

Walking until nightfall, a weary Kisa at last understood the meaning of Shakyamuni's words: Whoever is born has to one day die. There is no family that does not know the sorrow of parting from loved ones.

The young woman felt herself trembling like a leaf, then suddenly the need to find the mustard seed was gone. Kisa's eye to look at death had opened.

Kisa took her beloved child, which she had clasped to herself all those days and, leaving the child's body at the cemetery, returned to Shakyamuni and knelt before him.

Shakyamuni quietly asked her, "What has become of your beloved child? Did you find a mustard seed?"

Kisa spoke of the joy she experienced through awakening from her delusions, thanks to Shakyamuni's teaching. She asked to be made one of his disciples.

ℭℛ

To accept death and to realize we must die alone when the time comes: at a glance, these two things seem to be something we can deal with, or at least accept intellectually. When death hits close to home, though, it is difficult to face it calmly. Isn't this why we need religion in our lives?

27

What is the rationale against taking human life?

What is the rationale against taking human life? Mankind has long pondered this question.

When Shakyamuni commented on this problem, he did so in the following, easy-to-understand words,

> All beings tremble before violence.
>
> All fear death. All love life.
>
> See yourself in others.
>
> Then, whom can you hurt?
>
> What harm can you do?

> — *Dhammapada, Teachings of the Buddha* (Thomas Byrom Tr.) P. 8

When we consider, "see yourself in others," that is when we think we are like them, we can sense the solid basis underlying just how important it is to protect the lives of others.

Since ancient times, Buddhist philosophy has had a set of five precepts that places restrictions on what a human being can or cannot do. The first precept is against taking life. If there is no guarantee that human life is to be protected, then neither is there any guarantee that you will be allowed to live. If you want to live your life, then at the same time, you have to guarantee the lives of others will also be protected. This precept against killing, then, is man's most basic rule and is a strict standard by which we must all adhere.

Now, with regard to this problem, what strikes me as odd is this: why must we bring up the rationale against killing for discussion at all? Why must it be brought to our attention in the first place?

This problem of the rationale against killing may well be one that philosophers have long concerned themselves, but their insights have not trickled down into society in general, nor have they become a subject of further investigation. Clearly, this is still happening in society today.

I would contend, what we can single out as the cause for this odd state of affairs is that it arises from our lack of a real sense of life, apart from our usual sense of life in the abstract.

Not too long ago in Japan, when people were about to meet their end, they would request to die on their *tatami* mat, at home, rather than take their last breath on a cold hospital bed. In those days, the majority of people did just that: die in the home setting. Thus, when a person departed from this world, they did so holding the hands of their family members.

In those days, most families lived together, but the average life span was short, and it was not unusual for one to be present when a family member passed on. Ordinarily, it was much later when a person saw into the experience and was able to think it through.

How does death occur in society today?

First of all, in the modern household, we do not have the terminally ill patient. It is usually not at home but in a hospital that someone with a terminal illness will meet his end. While medical facilities have improved, as anyone who has been treated at a hospital can well attest, the fact is that dying in a hospital sharply reduces our chances to be present when someone dies.

Along with the aging of society, there is an increase in the number of elderly people, but there are very few households where three or more generations live together. Even though we may attend our grandpa's and grandma's funerals, it is rare that we are present to witness their final moments. In short, unlike the old days, the chances of seeing death firsthand, in the household setting, have been greatly reduced.

When we do not witness the event of death, we experience neither the sorrow or loneliness of death, nor the sense of loss that accompanies it. As a result, we grow up without any sense of how precious and noble life is.

One might say, to come to terms with death the heart has been marginalized.

In the past when death was not a distant event, but something one experienced immediately firsthand, there was no one who asked, "What is the rationale against killing?" There was no need to ask what everyone knew. Death was something everyone had experienced and knew for themselves.

In that sense, those who ask this question have already lost the ability to sense life. If someone has experienced the pain piercing one's heart, while witnessing the physical pain that accompanies death, one would not be asking such a question.

In Buddhism, *life* refers broadly to all forms of biological life, as well as the heart and mind of the human being. In the Buddhist way of thinking, one is blessed with life. It is not something that belongs to me personally. It is not something I possess. It is not something I am free to do with as I please. It is not to be treated as an object one buys or sells, or discards or picks up.

Behind every person who is born, there is a long stream of life, called the chain of life, which is necessary for that person to exist. Our parents, grandparents, and ancestors are all woven together into a tapestry of life that goes back in a continuous stream, and it is this stream of life that makes our lives possible.

We could well count the years since our mother gave birth to us, but it is also possible to conceive of our lives as the culmination of the past 3.5 billion years.

Furthermore, if we limit our scope to the present day, and think of the links that spread out laterally, there is not a single person who lives by himself. It is through our linkage to family and relatives, friends and companions, as well as others that we are able to live.

Moreover, if we think of our clothes, food, and shelter; there is nothing we have that did not depend on others. It is through the support of countless animals and plants that we are able to live.

Hatsuzo Ohsuga wrote a book called, *Life is Something We Share*, and in it appears the following words:

For man to live is not simply a matter of our having blood ties with our parents and siblings, we are also linked to the rest of the world. All living things born into this world, not just people, but animals and plants, coexist as a part of a greater life that they share.

When a person is killed, all these many links are suddenly broken. Therefore, life is not to be treated lightly.

28

Turning our thoughts to the life hereafter

The newspaper once carried this letter in its advice column:

Since a year ago, I have been giving death a lot of thought. I suppose that with each passing day, I am drawing closer to death, but I am not afraid to die. It is thinking of the physical and mental torment up to the point of death that keeps me up at night.

When I think that my children will one day die, I feel sorry for them. When I think that in the future they will not be able to have the situation to live a happy life, I worry and wonder why I ever gave birth to them. I try to change my mood, but can find no way to cheer myself, and so pass each day feeling blue. How can I live on the bright side? Please, tell me how to get a grip on my feelings.

There is a Latin saying, "*memento mori*," which means, "remember death," or "death should not be forgotten." In the Middle Ages, when Europe was devastated by plague and a great number of people died, these words were born. These words were, thus, used as a form of admonishment: in the midst of life, do not make light of death.

The fact that people of every age turn their thoughts to death is, I think, significant.

This is especially the case in our present society, where death is hidden from us. Since most cases of terminal illness are sent to medical facilities, even if you are a family member, there is virtually no chance for you to make your final amends.

Last year, my father died in June, at the age of 90. It is hard for anyone to lose a family member. However, through this experience, we become aware of things we had not noticed before. When someone we love dies, it is one of the greatest opportunities for us to learn about the undeniable reality of life.

If we are unaffected by death, we naturally do not turn our eyes to it. We live each day not thinking about death, and in a way, we might be happier, but when we are oblivious to death, we are missing something important in our lives.

Rennyo Shonin (the 8th Monshu of our Hongwanji) wrote, "The one great matter of our life hereafter." Our life hereafter refers to the world of life we will receive once our lives in this world come to an end. This is the one great issue we cannot lose sight of when living our lives. This expression is, thus, related to the words "memento mori," which was mentioned earlier.

"The one great issue of our life hereafter," confronts us with the question of life that transcends our regular life: "What will happen to us after we die, where will we go?" Are we to fall into hell, or are we to go into the ultimate bliss of the Pure Land? If we cannot resolve this question, there is no meaning to our lives in this world.

"The one great issue of our life hereafter," teaches that our thoughts on death and the meaning of life are two sides of the same coin. By thinking about death, a person's life will be enriched.

29

Your loved ones will always be close to you

A survey conducted in Japan, asked, "What do you associate the word Buddhism with?" By and large, the answers were "funeral services and memorial services."

At one time, the temple was a place where people went to renew their relationships with others, as well as the world. In the olden days, people went to the temple to listen to sermons, place their hands together in reverence, or participate in temple events.

Today, people go to the temple mostly for funerals and memorial services. More frequently, wedding ceremonies are held at Christian churches and hotels, and the first prayer of the New Year, as well as baby's 100th day, and children's 3rd, 5th and, 7th year birthdays are observed at Shinto shrines. Only funerals are largely conducted by the Buddhist denomination with which the family is traditionally associated.

Perhaps, it is due to this reason that Japanese people have the impression Buddhism is equated with the services for the deceased.

However, Buddhism as originally intended by Shakyamuni Buddha, began as a way of releasing the living person from suffering. That is, Buddhism was originally intended not for the sake of the deceased but for the sake of the living.

CR

I came across this poem by a mother who had lost her child.

How cold my cheeks
As I touch them with both my hands.
How thin the memories
As the third memorial comes to a close.

To paraphrase this poem:

When my beloved child passed away, I no longer wanted to live. Tears of grief streamed down my face. That was me two years ago. Now, for the third memorial service, I made the appointment at the temple, put together the guest list, arranged for the restaurant, ordered the sweets for everyone to take home. This is me now.

You might find yourself asking, where have all the sad

memories of that time gone? The memories of your grief have grown thin, which means the memories of your beloved have grown thin, and you feel a twinge of loneliness suddenly pass over you. I think these are the honest emotions this poem expresses.

ʚɞ

After a person dies, what remains?

All that is left are ashes and memories, some will say. You might say, all that remains of the body is the ashes, and all that remains of the heart is the memories.

The ashes are a tangible reminder of the deceased. The ashes and the grave where they are interred are, of course, important; but the ashes are not the person. It is not possible for those to be the same as when the person was alive.

Well, then, does that mean we have only memories to link us to the deceased?

No, it is possible for us to live along with the person we have lost.

When a person dies, he becomes Buddha. In Jodo Shinshu, while we are alive, we listen to the wishes of Amida Buddha and say the Nembutsu, and when our lives in this world come to an end, we are born into the Land of Amida Buddha.

Buddha is a force or functioning. You might compare it to the forces at work behind the changes of the seasons.

There is a children's song that goes, "Spring has come, spring has come! Oh, where has it come?" Spring itself cannot be seen with the eye. The water is warm, the sunlight is brighter, the cherry blossom buds are about to burst open, and we can feel the warm breeze blowing through the window. It is spring that makes us sense all of these forces at work, and so we know "spring has come." Where and when each person senses spring will differ; however, all will know of the arrival of spring. Spring's existence is something that everyone can verify for themselves.

The same is true for the Buddha. The Buddha is not an existence we know from some shape or form. The Buddha is something we come to sense after we build up a link to the Buddha, through the study of Buddhism, by attending the temple, and by observing the daily services at home.

The ashes and memories of the deceased are things of the past. The fact the deceased has become Buddha, to whom we can connect with our hearts, though, belongs to the present, the future, and forever. The Buddha is always with us.

 C3

When Shinran Shonin received word that his disciple in the Kanto area, Myoho-bo, had died, he sent a letter in return saying, "Ah, this is indeed wonderful!"

What Shinran Shonin wrote in that letter is as follows:

The very fact that we are brought around to encounter Namo Amida Butsu, means there is a rare and wonderful power at work.

Shinran Shonin is saying, there is a rare and wonderful force at work in life, through which we are brought to encounter the Nembutsu, Namo Amida Butsu. Although we say a person has departed, when a person had lived out the life in saying the Nembutsu, which is Namo Amida Bustsu, that person is then born into the Pure Land, through the power of Amida's Primal Vow. Since this is a buddha who has become one with Amida Buddha who saves all of us, we go even so far as to say, "Ah, this is indeed wonderful!"

The sadness of being unable to meet a departed loved one in this world is deep and consuming. On the other hand, our loved ones in Nembutsu are not lost in the world of delusions. When we consider they have "gone off to be born into the world of the Buddha," our hearts well up; in the midst of all the sadness, a feeling of gladness wells up in our hearts, expressed as, "Ah, this is indeed wonderful!"

30

No one is too young or too old to think about life

Letting your thoughts dwell on death has long been an important theme in Buddhism, ever since the time of Shakyamuni. This was not done to lessen the impact of this pressing problem people faced on a daily basis in the course of ordinary life. Nor was it to escape from some fearful destination in the life after death.

It was to see things from the perspective of death and then to return from that dimension to rethink the meaning of life. In this sense, death was grasped as the one great matter we had to deal with in life.

Today, I think we can say there is a tendency for many people to draw a line between "living" and "dying."

A great many young people think they are still standing at the beginning of life, from which point life is an uphill climb. For them, death is something wholly unrelated to them, hence they make no effort to give the matter any serious thought.

On the other end of the spectrum are the aged, who see themselves as approaching the final scene, with life going downhill from here on out. In that mind, they wonder how to pass the time until they die. Isn't this tendency one that we all share?

It does not matter whether you are young or old, one day is the same 24-hour length of time for everyone. Living that one day is the same for everyone, as it draws you one day closer to death. This fact is no different, whether you are a newborn or a person who has lived many decades. Whether you think of yourself as a person who is looking forward to life, or whether you think of yourself with only death awaiting you, there is no separation between these ways of thinking.

And so, there is no one who is ever too young to think about death, nor is there anyone who is too old to look toward the future with hope and to hold on to one's dreams.

Shinran's comment, "it is quite the same for all of us," shows that he thought of this problem at length. Just as a day is the same 24 hours, whoever you may be, it does not matter whether you are young or old, male or female, good or bad; Shinran arrived at the conclusion that all people equally enter the pathway of salvation.

That is why he guided others with the teaching that through shinjin (entrusting heart), when people depart from this world, they enter the Pure Land and become buddhas.

The view that, while in this world, it is impossible for us to attain satori, an awakening, through our own efforts: this is Jodo Shinshu. How much less suited are we to go out and save others? The reason is that as long as people have life left in them, it is impossible for human beings to ever free themselves entirely of their blind passions. We always seek to benefit ourselves.

What it really means to be saved in this world, is something that can wait until we are born into the Pure Land as buddhas. However, this present life is not a mere waiting room until that time. Each passing day is like a precious jewel, wrapped in the heart of Amida Buddha.

31

Birth in the Pure Land is cause for celebration

In the Indian language of Sanskrit, the term for "going to be born" is called *ut-pad*. This translates into English as the word "birth." This was translated into Chinese as *wangsheng*, "to go and be born." We go to the Pure Land to be born. From the world of human existence, we go to the world of the Buddha and are transformed.

There was someone who once asserted, "we do not die and then go to the Pure Land, but without dying, rather, we are born." This is the theory that between the two worlds of our defiled realm and the Pure Land, there is no time-and-space distinction. This would have to mean they are directly connected, since there is no interval between the two, or at least this seems to be strongly asserted.

CR

"Going to be born" might seem like an illogical expression, but it refers to the fact that from the world of human existence, we are born into the world of the Buddha. Since we can no longer enjoy the company of those who have departed, it is an occasion for sadness. However, when we remind ourselves that the departed have advanced to the world of the Buddha, freed of their blind passions, this is not an altogether sad occasion.

In Jodo Shinshu, satori does not mean to merely die and enter the world of enlightenment. Those who have gone do not simply go there and never come back; they also return to this world. The purpose of their return is to guide those left behind in this world, and to strive for their salvation. To be born into the Pure Land and to attain satori, means we are released from the bonds of our bind passions, and now being one with Amida Buddha, Ultimate Truth, we work for the salvation of others.

Shinran Shonin regarded his mentor Honen Shonin as one who had gone to the other shore and returned to this world. Shinran Shonin wrote in one of his *wasan* (poem):

> *Born on isolated islands,*
> *Scattered like millet in the sea,*
> *He spread the teaching of the Nembutsu;*
> *In order to guide sentient beings,*
> *He came into this world many times.*

— *Koso Wasan, Collected Works of Shinran, (CWS)* P. 390

Born in the country of Japan, whose islands are strewn like tiny millet seeds, Honen Shonin spread the teaching of the Nembutsu everywhere. Shinran Shonin praises Honen Shonin, saying he has returned to this world, over and over again, in order to guide others and save them.

Shinran Shonin also revered Honen Shonin as the manifestation of Bodhisattva Mahasthamaprapta, as well as that of Amida Buddha. For Shinran Shonin, in order for Honen Shonin to transmit Amida Buddha's wish and the teaching of the Nembutsu, that enlightened being had to have returned from the Pure Land to have such a profound effect on Shinran, who dwelt in this world.

By the time I had passed the age of 50, I had to bid farewell to many teachers and friends from my college days. I also had to say farewell to family members and relatives, one after another. It was a sad and difficult experience for me, and yet around this time, little by little, I began to feel a connection to the Pure Land.

Through the process of listening to the Dharma and reflecting on the Buddha and the Pure Land, a new way of looking at the world and what I should do in life arose in me. It was the workings of the truth of the Pure Land that opened up my path in life.

32

When hate is not avenged by hate, peace prevails

Some people say, whenever a war breaks out, you can bet religion will be involved. This is a view with which I beg to differ. It depends on how one defines religion, but those who reject religion or profess to be atheists will engage in struggle, as well.

When a war or disturbance actually occurs in the world, religion will often be involved. However, the cases where religion is the cause of war are few. It is possible to claim war erupts when people of different religions are living in close proximity to each other, but that alone does not lead to struggle. It is when there is a gap between the rich and poor, or when there is resentment or scorn of the other party or their culture—in short, when discrimination exists, the problems surface. Those problems fuse with the differences between their respective religions and turn into a disturbance.

When we examine its history, Buddhism cannot be said to be completely unrelated to war. In Jodo Shinshu, in the past, there was the uprising of the *Ikko-ikki*. It is impossible to tell how much this was a religious struggle, although the principals involved had deep roots in religion.

Further, with regard to World War II, it is an undeniable fact that the Buddhist denominations supported the war and cooperated with the war efforts.

Buddhism was originally a religion that worked to soothe our desires and anger. Buddhism sought this effect on an individual level—this is its basic approach. It was truly unfortunate that Buddhist teachings were unable to exert much effect on the war.

While this fact is one I deeply regret, as I learn anew to take responsibility for the past, I feel even more compelled to make an earnest wish for peace in this world.

ଓ

When World War II ended with the defeat of Japan, every country submitted their demands for reparations. At that time, Ceylon, (present day Sri Lanka) which was then under English rule, dismissed all claims for reparations. The Honorable J.R. Jayewardene, as the leader of the delegation from Ceylon to the San Francisco Peace Treaty, rose from his chair, and, citing the words of Shakyamuni that follow, made a stirring speech urging all countries to put aside their claims for reparation.

For hatred does not cease by hatred at any time: hatred
ceases by love, this is an old rule.

—*Dhammapada*, (Max Mueller Tr.) P. 8

I think it is about time people recognize the compassionate
support Buddhists provided to the rebuilding of Japan during
the postwar era.

CR

At present, there are people who are losing their lives in wars
around the world.

In a normal society, if a person takes the life of another, it is
considered a crime. In the state of war, however, when one person kills another he becomes a hero. Thus, war is a most
hideous state of affairs.

Whatever way you look at it, this paradox does not make
sense, but in many countries, ethics and politics do not match
up, which is the sad reality.

All men tremble at punishment, all men love life; remember that thou art like unto them, and do not kill, nor cause
slaughter.

—*Dhammapada*, (Max Mueller Tr.) P. 8

However outstanding the reason, there is simply no justifi-
cation for taking the life of another. Another's way of life or
way of thinking may be fundamentally different than your
own, but that is no reason to take a life. Life is precious.

We are the recipients of the immeasurable compassion of
Amida Buddha, who will not rest until all living things are
saved.

If people are being crushed by sadness and suffering, I will take my place alongside them and live with them, our hearts beating each second as one — this is the Buddha's wish.

At the time shinjin becomes settled, birth too becomes settled

—*Collected Works of Shinran (CWS)*, P. 523

33

Say Namo Amida Butsu as if you were saying "Hello" to the Buddha

Namo Amida Butsu: Do you know what it means?

Namo Amida Butsu has its origins in Namo-A-mita-Buddha, a saying that appears in the sutras of India. Namo means, "I put my trust in you, I will follow you, I entrust my life to you." A-mita-Buddha means the Buddha that cannot be measured. What is it that cannot be measured? It is this Buddha's light and life. Immeasurable light symbolizes a light that will not be stopped from reaching those in despair. Immeasurable life expresses the life that transcends time. In other words, we can think of A-mita, or Amida Buddha, as the Buddha not limited by time or space, who illuminates us constantly, wherever we may go.

Namo Amida Butsu thus expresses the feeling, "I entrust everything to Amida Buddha."

ᘓ

"I am not able to say the Nembutsu naturally and spontaneously. What can I do about it?"

There are people who ask me such questions.

I first suggest to these people to say the Nembutsu casually, as if they were simply saying, "Hello," to Amida Buddha. When you first start out, it is better not to get bogged down in questions of why you are doing this, or where it will all lead.

There are, of course, clear-cut answers to these questions, but that does not mean it will lead you to say the Nembutsu more easily or naturally.

The word "Namo" shares the same origins with the word *"Namaste,"* used in India and Nepal today. Namaste is a greeting used as "Good day" or "Welcome" or "Goodbye." So, without thinking too deeply about it, try to say Namo Amida Butsu as if it were a comfortable way of greeting Amida Buddha.

As a greeting, it is not necessary for Namo Amida Butsu to be enunciated crisply down to the very last syllable. Namo Amida Butsu, down through the ages, has transformed itself and is now being expressed as *Naman dabutsu* and *Naman dabu.* Similarly, there is no difference whether you call your mother: Mom, Mommy, or Mama; they all point to the same person. It is more important for you to feel comfortable saying it.

I have heard that native English speakers have a lot of trouble saying *Namo-Amida-Butsu.* If a person finds themselves awkwardly pronouncing the Nembutsu, it doesn't matter. You should just think that the heart of Amida Buddha is the heart to save all without exception. This heart of Amida Buddha already exists in the depths of our own hearts.

When you start saying the Nembutsu, rather than asking a lot of difficult questions about it, it is better to just start saying the Nembutsu in your own way. Then learn about Buddhism gradually, as you go along. Somewhere along the way, you will discover the Nembutsu is more than just a word of greeting.

A person does not use the Nembutsu as a means to make

their wishes come true. When you become a person who is able to say the Nembutsu, that means you are a person who can sense the presence of Amida Buddha. It is important we come to say the Nembutsu naturally and spontaneously.

34

It is a great comfort to know someone is always calling out to us

When you become a person who senses the presence of Amida Buddha in your life, you will say the Nembutsu naturally and spontaneously.

Sensing the presence of Amida Buddha, you will realize the Nembutsu you have been saying is not just a word of greeting, it is Amida Buddha calling to you.

Does it then mean Amida Buddha is responding to my request to save me? No, that is not the case. Amida Buddha is calling to us from even before that time, saying, "There is no need to worry, leave it all to me." Namo Amida Butsu is Amida Buddha urging us to "leave it all to me."

When our Nembutsu, which started out as a greeting to the Buddha, becomes natural and spontaneous, we realize Amida Buddha has been calling to us from long before. We are always Amida Buddha's deepest concern. When we realize that, we say, "Thank you," with a heart full of gratitude.

That is the Nembutsu.

CR

Have you ever run into an old friend, in some unexpected place, and while remembering old times, you smile and exchange greetings?

You might be at a crowded station, or busy department store, when all of a sudden, someone calls to you. When that happens, I think most people at that moment will feel a sense of comfort. Until that time, you are being jostled about in a crowd of strangers, and then you run into someone who knows you, and this eases some of your tension. It might be someone who is just an acquaintance, but you find yourself breaking out in a smile and exchanging greetings and pleasantries.

We are born alone and we die alone. While we are alive, we give support to and receive support from countless others, and it is through this mutual support that we manage to live. In a crowd of strangers at a station or department store, it is only natural that we are on guard to protect ourselves; hence, our hearts are closed to those around us. When we happen to meet someone who knows us, though, it releases the tension in our hearts. That is, when we meet someone who knows us, when we come into contact with someone who is calling to us, we experience a sense of relief—isn't this true?

In the course of our busy lives, we experience all kinds of sufferings, anxieties, and loneliness. We have to walk life's path, burdened with sorrows. However, there is someone who watches over us as we walk along, who makes our situation his primary concern, who keeps calling to us. Just to know someone is there for us is a great comfort, putting our hearts at ease. That someone is Amida Buddha.

35

Shinjin (entrusting heart) is something we receive from the Buddha

No matter what religion or denomination, it is important to believe. When you cannot believe the person you are talking to, you don't even feel like listening to them. Belief or trust is a necessary prerequisite to learning something. In a sense, belief or faith is the starting point of Buddhism.

In the Jodo Shinshu tradition, this frame of mind is important as a starting point. But Jodo Shinshu then reflects on this mind to its deepest level and calls it shinjin (entrusting heart). The words, "Shinjin is all that matters," reflects how much importance we place on it.

The word shinjin, when used in general, is often used as a verb, as in the sentence "to believe with all my heart." In this case, it means the state of your heart remains unchanged as you count on the gods or buddhas to grant your wishes.

In contrast, when the word shinjin is used as a noun, as in Jodo Shinshu, it means my heart has been transformed into a heart that entrusts. It points to a change that has come over my heart.

In India, the word shinjin conveyed the meaning of a heart that had received the Three Treasures: Buddha, Dharma, and Sangha, which is the heart that had attained purity and grasped the teachings. In the Buddhist tradition since, many people have sought to attain awakening to ultimate truth.

Shinran Shonin was one of these people. Shinran Shonin reflected on what he had learned of the Pure Land teachings from his predecessors. He looked at the way of life within the age and society in which he lived, and then he looked deep within himself. In that reflection, he realized human beings are not made to uphold precepts. We embrace our blind passions and are unable to sever our desires and delusions. Ours is an existence dragged down into the whirlpool of our own egos. As far as awakening to shinjin on our own, we are too entrenched in blind passions to be able to do so. Shinran Shonin realized it was impossible to expect the Buddha to save us if everything was dependent on our awakening to shinjin first.

Imagine if you faced an insurmountable problem, like the loss of a beloved child, or the uncertainty that you might not live until tomorrow. Even if told, "Purify your heart and become a good person! Get rid of your blind passions!" you could not do it. That is because the heart is caught up in its own peculiar way of doing things. When we are faced with an insurmountable problem, we are given an opportunity to look deep into ourselves, into the way our hearts are. We realize it is no easy matter to control our hearts. A clean and pure heart does not emerge from within us.

Amida Buddha asks no questions whatsoever as to our abilities or whether our hearts are good or bad. Whatever kind of person we might be, whether we are bright or slow, young or old, good or evil; the compassion of Amida Buddha shines its light on everyone, rejecting none. If our hearts became pure, there would be no need for the Buddha to save us. Amida Buddha takes those of us who are without pure hearts and extends to us his heart of ultimate reality. We receive that heart when the light of Amida Buddha shines upon us—that is shinjin.

For those of us who belong to the Jodo Shinshu tradition, we regard shinjin as something that has been given to us from Amida Buddha. Because it is a gift initiated from the side of Amida Buddha, we use expressions like, "We receive shinjin," or "shinjin that is given to us."

In Japanese, when we speak about shinjin in the Jodo Shinshu tradition, we often add an honorific prefix, "*go*" to the word shinjin, (*goshinjin*). This is because shinjin is not something we create ourselves, but something we have been blessed by Amida Buddha. Shinjin is given to us by the power of the Buddha (*tariki*—Other Power)

Small children and babies are unable to do things on their own and must leave everything to their mothers. My relationship to Amida Buddha is like that. The reason small children can leave everything to their mothers is their mothers are constantly calling to them, worried about them, ready to nurse them, change their diapers, and do whatever it takes to care for them. It is from this nurturing that a sense of security is born in the child. We might say, the child's sense of relief is something the mother gives to the child. Here, the child's stage of development, level of ability, or whether the child's heart is good or bad is not a problem at all to the loving mother.

For Shinran Shonin, shinjin is the sole cause for attaining birth in the Pure Land and awakening to enlightenment. When we leave everything to the compassion of Amida Buddha, then "shinjin is all that matters" and we are saved.

It is through receiving Amida Buddha's true heart that I feel this imperfect self of mine being embraced in the compassion of Amida Buddha. That is where I find an indescribable feeling of joy and peace of mind. The manifestation of shinjin is the Nembutsu, Namo Amida Butsu.

36

All things are interconnected with one another. This truth is called pratitya-samutpada

One day, Rennyo Shonin picked up a piece of paper lying in the hallway and said, "These things are all the property of the Buddha. We should think twice before letting them go to waste." What Rennyo Shonin wants to tell us is even a scrap of paper belongs to the world of the Buddha, so we should not be wasteful. This does not apply to paper alone. Rennyo Shonin is saying, all things must be treated with care and not merely hungrily consumed to no purpose.

Among the basic tenets of Buddhism is the teaching of *pratitya-samutpada*: all things are interdependent, interconnected, and intricately joined together. While this is true of human life, it is also true of life outside the human sphere, as well as things outside of life itself, with nature as a whole being connected in this way—this is the truth of pratitya-samutpada.

Even in this single piece of paper, there are the lives of the plants that made up the raw material, and to turn that raw material into paper, there was the work of many hands. Further, in order for the paper to be delivered to you, it involved numerous other people. The fact that the paper is on the table before you means a lot of causes and conditions had to be fulfilled in order for it to happen. For that reason, while we may be talking only of a single sheet of paper, we must not be negligent of this aspect of things. When you let your thoughts turn to the links by which this paper reached you, you become aware of how it is linked to all things, and once you know that, you could never let it go to waste.

In this way, whatever it may be, there is not one thing in all existence that exists individually: all things are connected, linked to one another, and therefore they "are"—this is the pratitya-samutpada way of thinking.

Pratitya-samutpada, thus, offers a valuable way of looking at things when we seek to address today's problems of environmental destruction, armed military conflict, and other events where countless lives are lost; not merely human lives alone.

With regard to pratitya-samutpada, this interconnectedness does not only mean the blood ties of parent and child, or brother and sister, that bind people together. It points to our friends and colleagues who give us mutual support, and also to those who, at first glance, seem to have no relationship to us. Some kind of tie exists: this is the teaching of pratitya-samutpada.

Shinran Shonin left these words for us,

> 'As for me, Shinran, I have never said the Nembutsu even once for the repose of my departed father and mother. For all sentient beings, without exception, have been our parents and brothers and sisters in the course of countless lives in many states of existence. On attaining Buddhahood after this present life, we can save every one of them.'
>
> —*A Record in Lament of Divergences, (CWS)*, P. 664

In other words, "I have never once said the Nembutsu for the sake of my late father and mother. The reason I do not do so is, in the course of rebirth that all forms of life undergo, we have all been bonded to one another as father or mother or sister or brother." It is important to cherish all of life as our mothers and fathers and sisters and brothers, not just our own parents. And he explains to us that, wherever they may be, once one becomes a buddha, one will be in a position to go to their loved one's aid.

It is not that only those who are related to us are saved. It is also not the case that only human beings are saved. All life must be saved. To save all, is the reason for Amida Buddha's existence. This is how Shinran Shonin thinks and feels.

When this vast and great vow of Amida Tathagata touches our hearts, one does not think, "Well, as long as I am happy, that's all that matters, who cares about the rest?"—This is the thinking of someone who is shut up in his own world, and has lost sight of pratitya-samutpada. He has yet to realize he is caught up in the state of ignorance.

Don't think in the narrow sense of just those closest to you, with yourself at the center. Think more expansively of your connectedness to life. After all, we are in the same boat as beings who Amida Buddha intends to save.

All things, the water and the air included, are linked together, one thing encircling and being encircled by the other. The mountain and the river bestow me with so many blessings. When Amida Buddha shines upon me and all of the rest of life, we are linked together as lives saved by that light. All things on earth, all things in the universe, are in the fold of this great life-force linking us all together.

In this world, there is no life that was ever lived in vain. There is no life that is meaningless. All life is linked together. All of us share in the light that Amida Buddha shines upon us—this is what Buddhism teaches.

Epilogue

When I was in high school, I came across a passage in my English textbook that read, "Man is the primate of all creation." Before I could even begin to understand what the English meant, first I had to make sense of what the Japanese version of it was getting at, and I remember being stuck at that point. Checking the dictionary it said, "Man is the highest form of existence, possessed of mysterious and superior powers." It is indeed the case that man, compared to other creatures, is in possession of superior abilities, but looking at man from another perspective, we cannot fail to observe how powerfully he is swayed by his desires, and how greatly he suffers and worries over things beyond his control.

Buddhism teaches that there is a way to resolve the problem of the blind passions that lie at the foundation of human suffering, and has made this its teaching for the past two thousand five hundred years. Mankind, today, has mastered scientific technology so as to amplify mankind's desires. Thus, I feel it my mission in life to draw from the marrow of the Buddhist teachings, as ancient as they may appear to be, and to present its message far and wide. It is my greatest hope that by publishing this book, those who are weary from the tedium of everyday life, who are dissatisfied with their lives, who are unhappy and think they deserve better, will discover in themselves the joy and meaning of life.

Monshu Koshin Ohtani
Spring 2003

Sources

Asada Shosaku (b. 1919), *Following the Way of Bone: A Volume of Nembutsu Poetry/Kotsudo o yuku: Nembutsu shishu*, Kyoto: Hozokan, 1988.

Hayashima Kyosho (1922–2000), *Gautama Buddha/ Gotama Buddha*, Tokyo: Iwanami Gakujutsu Bunko, 1990
— *Nembutsu Issa: the Poet Kobayashi Issa: The Secret of His Gentleness/ Nembutsu Issa: Haijin Kobayashi Issa: Sono yasashisa no himitsu*, Tokyo: Shikisha.

Ikeda Gyoshin (b. 1953), *Modern Society and Jodo Shinshu/ Gendai shakai to Jodo Shinshu*, Kyoto: Hozokan, 2000.

Kakehashi Jitsuen (b. 1927), Contributor, *Hotoke to hito dai 7-go (journal)*, *Mumyokai-dojin hen*, Kyoto: Nagata Bunshodo, 1989.

Matsuno-o Choon (1923–1999), *Buddhism and Jodo Shinshu/ Bukkyo to Jodo Shinshu*, Kyoto: Hongwanji Shuppan, 1992).

Max Muller, Friedrich (1823–1900), Tr., *The Dhammapada: a Collection of Verses, Sacred Books of the East Vol. 10*, Oxford: Clarendon Press, 1881.

Miyagi Shizuka (b. 1931), *The World of the Ultimate/ Mujo no sekai, Gendai no Shinshu series*, Kyoto: Yayoi Shobo, 1980.

Murakami Shijimi (1897–), *Grass Flute/ Kusabue*, Osaka: Seikoh-sha, 1977.

Murakami Sokusui (1919–2000), *The Mistaken and Correct*

Understanding of Shinran Doctrine/ Shinran kyogi no gokai to rikai, Kyoto: Nagata Bunshodo, 1984.

Nakamura Hajime (1912–1999), *The Buddha's Words of Truth and Words of Encouragement/ Buddha no shinri no kotoba: Buddha no kankyo no kotoba*, Tokyo: Iwanami Bunko, 1978.
—*Gautama Buddha: The Life of Shakyamuni/ Gotama Buddha: Shakuson den*, Kyoto: Hozokan, 1958; rev. 1974.
—*The Words of the Buddha/ Buddha no kotoba*, Tokyo: Iwanami Bunko, 1985.

Ohsuga Hatsuzo (b. 1923), *Life is Something We Share/ Inochi wakeai-shi mono*, Tokyo: Hakujusha, 1987.

Ohtani Koshin (b. 1945), Tr. *The Buddha's Wish for the World*, (*Ashita ni wa kogan arite* Tokyo: Kadokawa, 2003) New York: American Buddhist Study Center Press, 2009.

The Shin Buddhism Translation Series, H. Inagaki, Ed. *The Three Pure Land Sutras, Volume I: The Amida Sutra and the Contemplation Sutra*, Kyoto: Jodo Shinshu Hongwanji-ha, 2003
—*The Three Pure Land Sutras, Volume II: The Sutra on the Buddha of Immeasurable Life*, Kyoto: Jodo Shinshu Hongwanji-ha, 2009

Shinran Shonin (1173–1263) et al., *The Collected Works of Shinran*, Nagao Gadjin, Ed., Kyoto: Jodo Shinshu Hongwanji-ha, 1997.
—*The Jodo Shinshu Sacred Works: Annotated ed./ Jodo Shinshu Seiten: Chushaku-ban*, Jodo Shinshu Seiten Hensan Iinkai, comp., Kyoto: Hongwanji Shuppan, 1988.

Shohi Tetsuo (b. 1919), *The Awakening to an Existence Bound to Die/ Shi subeki mi no mezame*, Kyoto: Hozokan, 1995.

— *Living Together with Death/ Shi to tomo ni ikiru*, Kyoto: Hozokan, 1995.

— *On the Fact that I am Human: Vol. 1/ Ningen de aru koto: 1*, Kyoto: Hozokan, 1988.

Uryuzu Ryushin (b. 1932), *Hosokawa Gyoshin (1926–2007), Shinshu sho jiten*, Kyoto: Hozokan, 1987.

Woodward, Frank L. (1870–1952), Tr., *The Book of the Gradual sayings (Anguttara-nikaya) or more-numbered suttas*, London: Pali Text Society by Oxford University Press, 1932.

Acknowledgment

I am deeply grateful to Gomonshu Koshin Ohtani and the Nishi Hongwanji International Department, as well as all those that have worked so hard in the translation, editing, and printing of this book. This is a very special book in so many ways, including being the first book that Gomonshu Ohtani has given permission to be translated and published into English.

I would like to thank Reverend Michio Tokunaga, *Kangaku*, (Hongwanji scholar) Jodo Shinshu Hongwanji-ha, International Department in Kyoto, Japan, for requesting American Buddhist Study Center (ABSC) to edit, publish, and distribute an English translation of the book *Ashita ni wa kogan arite*. We are deeply grateful to Tokunaga-Sensei for giving us this important assignment, as this book is dedicated to the 750th memorial of Shinran Shonin.

I would also like to thank Wayne Yokoyama for his excellent translation of *Ashita ni wa kogan arite*. He has helped to create a smooth editing process. *The Buddha's Wish for the World* publication committee is deeply grateful to Yokoyama-Sensei for his translation and guidance on expressions used in this book.

The editing of this book has been a monumental undertaking with so many dedicated Jodo Shinshu Buddhists involved. The first round of editing was done at the Honpa Hongwanji Mission in Honolulu under the guidance of Reverend Tatsuo Muneto, Director for the Buddhist Study Center. The final editing was handled by Reverend Marvin Harada, minister of Orange County Buddhist Church and its

Buddhist Education Center (BEC). Reverend John Paraskevopoulos in Australia also put together the first draft of edits.

A very special thank you to poet Cathy Song, member of the Buddhist Study Center in Honolulu, for her contributions towards the editing of this book.

Reverend Marvin Harada together with his editors skillfully captured the warmth and depths of Gomonshu's wisdom and compassion. Special thanks to Reverend Mutsumi Wondra, Arlene Kato, Kimberly Kearns, Kay Mitchell, and Ron Taber.

In one sense, Harada-Sensei and his editors had the hardest assignment for they had to labor through all the existing edits and come up with the final version.

Arlene Kato not only helped in the editing, she also designed and created the beautiful cover and formatted this book. Arlene is a gifted artist and I am happy that she was able to take on this project.

Three more major participants in the development of this book include Dr. Alfred Bloom, Dr. Gordon Bermant and Ms. Patricia Barry. Dr. Bloom, a member of the Buddhist Study Center, Honolulu, helped Muneto-Sensei with the editing and gave us many good suggestions. Dr. Bermant was very helpful in keeping this project on track and on time, writing articles, and helping with fundraising. Ms. Barry assisted me with the initial public relation funding campaign.

In Gassho,
Hoshin Seki
President, American Buddhist Study Center,
New York

Special Thank You

With deep appreciation, thank you to the many people who helped us fund the Gomonshu's book. Our goal was to raise funds for a national publicity campaign to introduce Shin Buddhism and Monshu Koshin Ohtani. It was through your donations that we can celebrate not only in our Jodo Shinshu community, but also in those communities whose lives will be enriched by the Gomonshu's wisdom. We are especially grateful to the following individuals, temples, foundations, and organizations for their contributions.

Individuals

Dr. Richard and Thelma Ando	Rev. Akio and Tamiko Miyaji
Jeffrey and Namy Folick	Gary Moriwaki
Rev. Marvin and Gail Harada	Hoshin and Josephine Seki
Raymond and Miyoko Itaya	LT Jeanette Shin
Hiroji Kariya	Rev. Fumiaki and Rev. Patricia Usuki
Masaru and Sakaye Kato	Rev. Jim Yanagihara
Roy and Yasuko Kato	Anonymous

Past Buddhist Churches of America Presidents

Dr. Gordon Bermant	Mr. Hiroji Kariya	Mr. Sei Shohara
Mr. Noboru Hanyu	Mr. Milnes Kurashige	Mr. Ralph Sugimoto, Jr.
Mr. Walter Hashimoto	Mr. Ryo Munekata	Mr. M. Uchiyama
Mr. George Iseri	Mr. Kiyoshi Naito	Mr. Steve Yamami
Mr. Douglas Iwamoto	Mr. Herbert Osaki	Mr. James Yoshimura

Temples

Arizona Buddhist Temple

Buddhist Church of Oakland

Honpa Hongwanji Mission of
of Hawai'i

Idaho-Oregon Buddhist Temple

Jodo Shinshu Buddhist Temples
of Canada

Lahaina Hongwanji Mission

Midwest Buddhist Temple

Mountain View Buddhist Temple

New York Buddhist Church

Nishi Hongwanji

Orange County Buddhist Church

Oregon Buddhist Temple

Palo Alto Buddhist Temple

San Fernando Valley
Hongwanji Buddhist Temple

San Jose Buddhist Church Betsuin

Foundations and Organizations

Aratani Foundation

Buddhist Churches of America

Bukkyo Dendo Kyokai

Eastern District Council

International Association
of Buddhist Culture

Orange County Buddhist Church

Orange County Buddhist Church
Buddhist Education Center

Rev. Kono Scholarship Fund

San Fernando Valley
Hongwanji Buddhist Temple
Buddhist Women's Association

Unno Family Sudhana Fund